Australian Signpost MATHS

1

Mentals

Alan McSeveny Diane McSeveny-Foster Rachel McSeveny

Introduction

Using the Mentals Books

Each unit of the Mentals Book is programmed to review content from the previous two units of the Student Book. For example, Mentals Book Unit 5 can be used to review Student Book Units 3 and 4 while Student Book Unit 5 is being taught. Unit 5 from both books should be completed in the same week.

Presentation

- The content of the strands Number and Algebra, Measurement and Geometry, and Statistics and Probability is covered thoroughly.
- Essential skills are explained.
- Language, graphs, problem solving and tables are given a high profile.
- Mathematics is applied to real-life situations wherever possible.

Mixed-topic Questions

The units present questions in a mixed-topic format.

- This is essential for thorough understanding and continuous review.
- It will allow the teacher to discover weaknesses that could otherwise pass unnoticed.
- The approach reflects real life – similar questions don't often occur together.
- It provides a real test of understanding.

If You Do Not Use a Student Book

This book will be invaluable to those who do not use a Student Book, as it ensures both thorough coverage and constant review of the syllabus content.

ID Cards

- The ID Cards on pages 4 and 5 review the terms essential to success in this course.
- These cards can be used over and over again to improve understanding.

You can't do the maths if you don't know the language!

Multiple-choice Questions

The multiple-choice questions on page 70 introduce a variety of question types.

- Three headers on each double-page spread provide an opportunity for discussion. Suggestions on how to use them in the classroom are given on page 3.
- Cartoons make mathematics more appealing.
- Two lizards are hidden on each page for students to find.
- The third section of each unit usually contains counting exercises in the border.

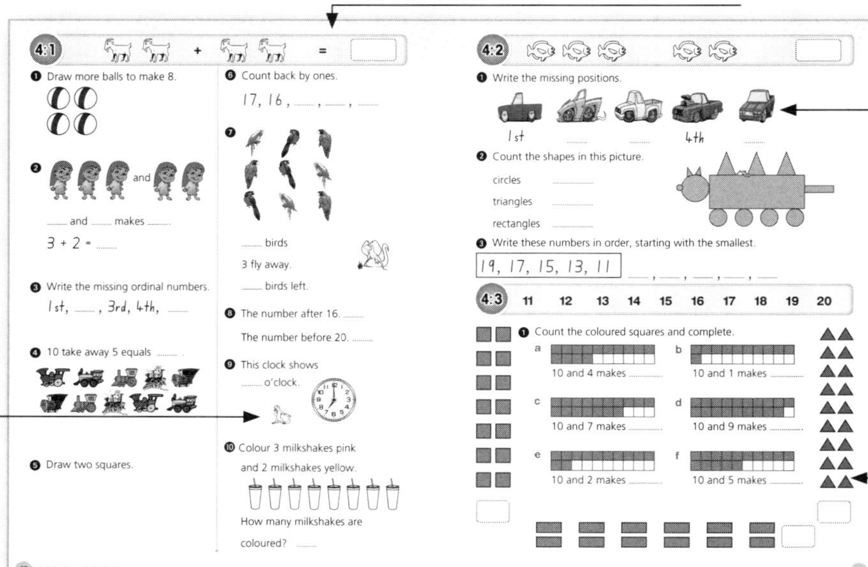

 ISBN 978 1 4886 2177 2

1 Contents

Unit Header Activities

1:1	Count the tomatoes (Q2).	**1:2**	Count the beetles.	**1:3**	Count the strawberries.
2:1	Count the scooters (Q5).	**2:2**	Count the horses.	**2:3**	Numbers 1–10
3:1	Count the tomatoes (Q12).	**3:2**	Count the frogs.	**3:3**	Position of animals
4:1	2 + 2 = 4 (Q2,10)	**4:2**	3 + 2 = 5	**4:3**	Numbers 11–20
5:1	Circle the 1st car. Cross the last.	**5:2**	Name shapes/Discuss pattern (Q1).	**5:3**	2 + 8
6:1	Circle one half of the pictures (Q5).	**6:2**	Colour half of each shape.	**6:3**	4 + 7
7:1	10 take away 7 (Q5).	**7:2**	Draw a line to show half (Q3).	**7:3**	Say the time on the clocks.
8:1	Discuss and complete the pattern.	**8:2**	8 – 2	**8:3**	Double 2.
9:1	3 and 2 makes 5 (Q2, 12)	**9:2**	10 + 4 (Q2)	**9:3**	Double 10 (Q1).
10:1	Discuss heavy and light things (Q9).	**10:2**	4 + 5 (Q1)	**10:3**	Double 3.
11:1	5 + 4 (Q1, 7)	**11:2**	Count by 10s.	**11:3**	Join the dots.
12:1	How many squares in the pattern?	**12:2**	Count the buttons by 1s or 2s.	**12:3**	Name 2D shapes. Discuss pattern.
13:1	8 – 5 (Q1, 8)	**13:2**	Which of these objects roll?	**13:3**	What is on the left?
14:1	8 – 3	**14:2**	Numbers 1–6	**14:3**	Count on 4. 5 + 4
15:1	How many sides/corners?	**15:2**	Write the numbers modelled (Q2).	**15:3**	10 – 4
16:1	Which holds the most? (Q2, 7)	**16:2**	Write the number modelled (Q1).	**16:3**	Write the numbers modelled.
17:1	Ordinals and shapes (Q9)	**17:2**	3 + 7	**17:3**	10 + 10
18:1	Discuss and complete the pattern.	**18:2**	6 – 3	**18:3**	Write the numbers modelled.
19:1	3 + 5 (Q2)	**19:2**	Describe each object (Q1).	**19:3**	2D shapes, 3 + 3 + 3
20:1	Circle half of the toys (Q2).	**20:2**	Full, half full, empty	**20:3**	9 – 4
21:1	Number pattern (Q6, 7)	**21:2**	4 + 6	**21:3**	Shade half of each shape.
22:1	7 – 5 (Q1, 11)	**22:2**	What numbers add to give 7?	**22:3**	3 + 3 + 3 (3 groups of 3)
23:1	Which objects can stack?	**23:2**	Number pattern (Count by 10s.)	**23:3**	Join the dots. (Count by 2s.)
24:1	Discuss the patterns.	**24:2**	6 + 4 (Q1)	**24:3**	Join the dots. (Count by 2s.)
25:1	Circle half of this collection.	**25:2**	How many tens?	**25:3**	Number pattern (Count by 10s.)
26:1	9 – 3 (Q6)	**26:2**	Months of the year (Q1, 3)	**26:3**	How many dots on each dice?
27:1	6 + 3 (Q2)	**27:2**	Describe these 3D objects.	**27:3**	What is the total on each domino?
28:1	How many more on the right?	**28:2**	9 – 4	**28:3**	Count by 2s to find the total.
29:1	Describe the pattern.	**29:2**	Months of the year (Q1)	**29:3**	10 – 3
30:1	6 – 3 (Q1, 8)	**30:2**	Discuss position.	**30:3**	Complete the number patterns.
31:1	How many more on the left?	**31:2**	Months of the year	**31:3**	7 + 8
32:1	Discuss the pattern.	**32:2**	Circle the heavier sides.	**32:3**	Describe the 2D shapes.

ID Card A

Do not write on this card.

ID Card A

1
+
a__________

2
−
s__________

3
=
is e________ to

4
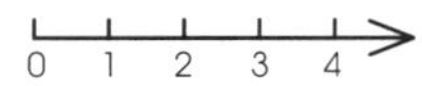

n________ line

5
1st, 2nd, 3rd, 4th …
o________ numbers

6
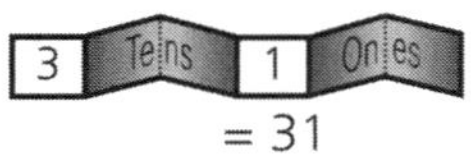

n__________ expander

7
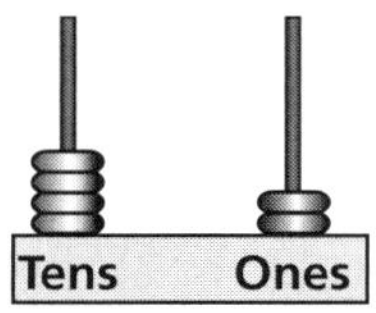

a________

8

o_____ b_______

9
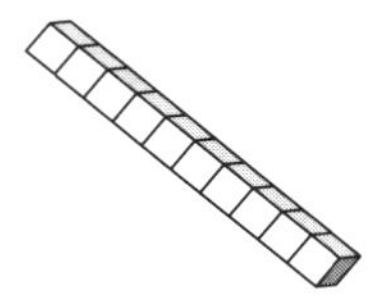
t_____ b_______

10
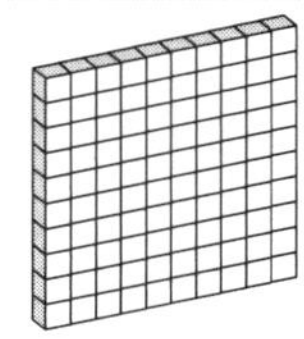
h__________ b________

11
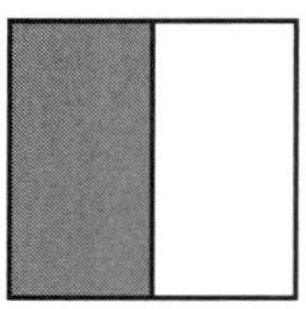
$\frac{1}{2}$
h__________

12
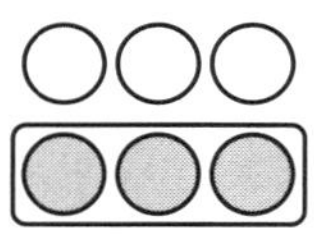
$\frac{1}{2}$
h__________

13
$
d__________

14
c
c__________

15

__________coin

16

__________coin

17

__________coin

18

__________coin

19

__________coin

20

__________coin

21

__________note

22

__________note

23

__________note

24

__________note

25

__________note

26
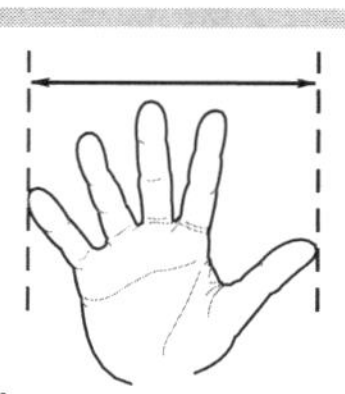
h________ s________

27

equal arm b________

28

d________time

29

o'________

30

h_____ p_____

See page A1 for answers

 ISBN 978 1 4886 2177 2

ID Card B

Do not write on this card.

1

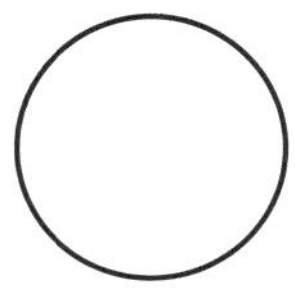

c__________

2

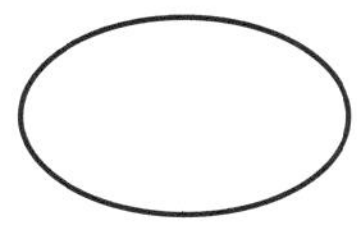

o__________

3

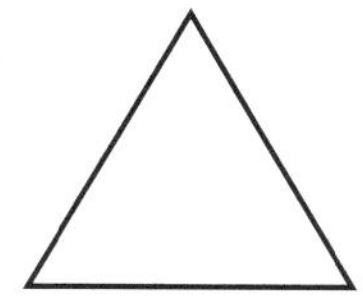

t__________

4

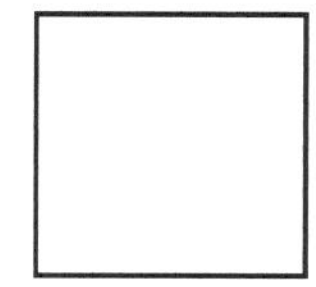

s__________

5

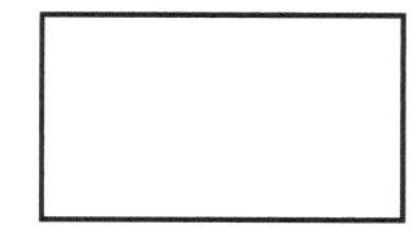

r__________

6

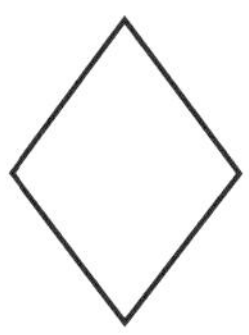

r__________

7

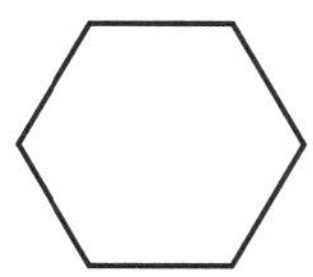

h__________

8

s__________ line

9

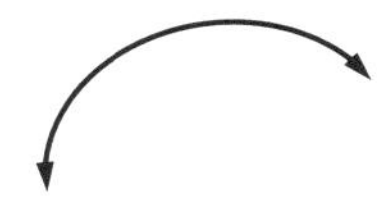

c__________ line

10

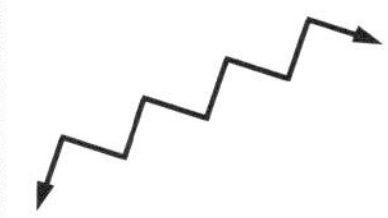

z__________ line

11

b__________ line

12

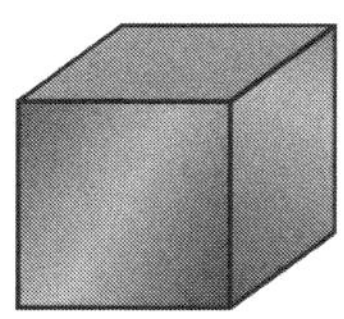

c__________

13

s__________

14

c__________

15

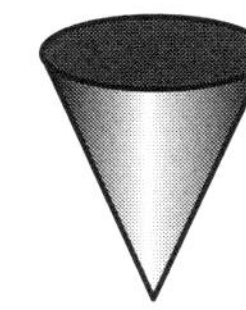

c__________

16

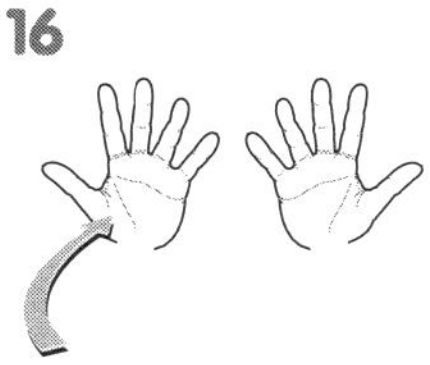

l__________ hand

17

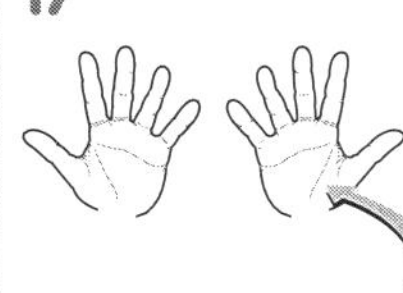

r__________ hand

18

a__________

19

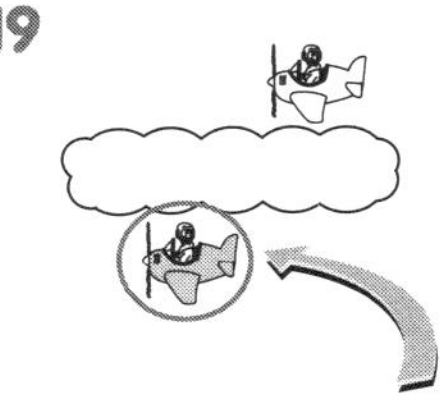

b__________

20

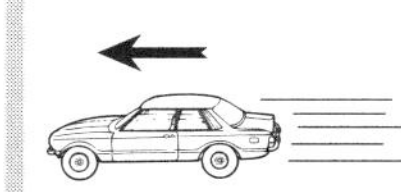

f__________

21

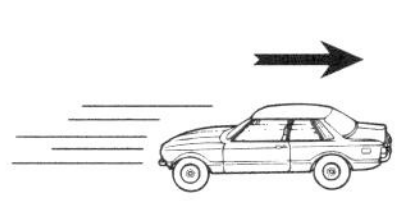

b__________

22

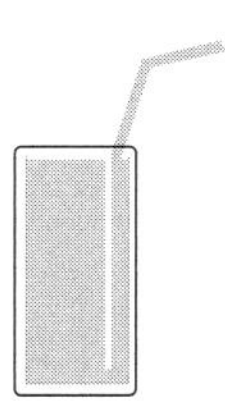

f__________

23

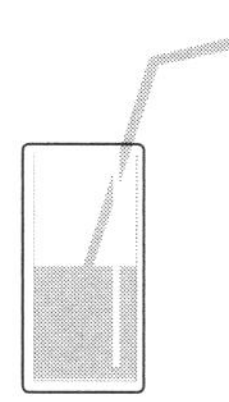

half f__________

24

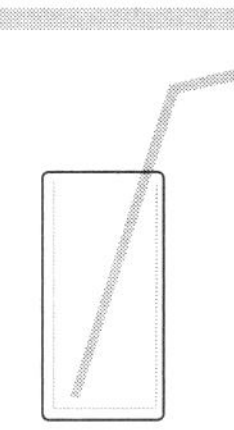

e__________

25

l__________

26

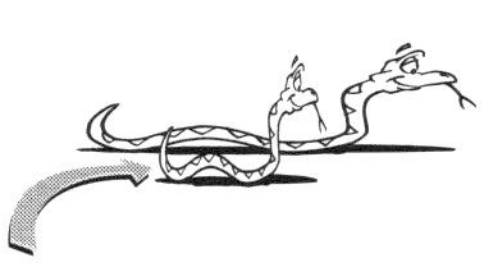

s__________

27

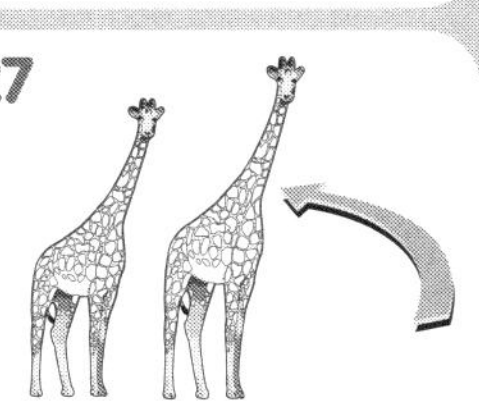

t__________

28

h__________

29

l__________

30

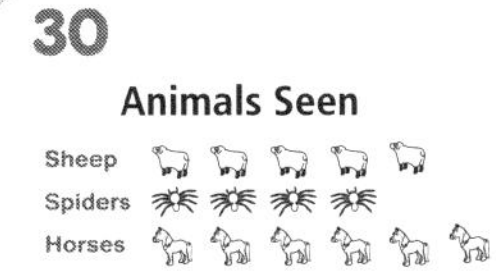

p__________
g__________

See page A1 for answers

1 7 tomatoes. I ate 3.

How many are left? ______

2 How many altogether? ______

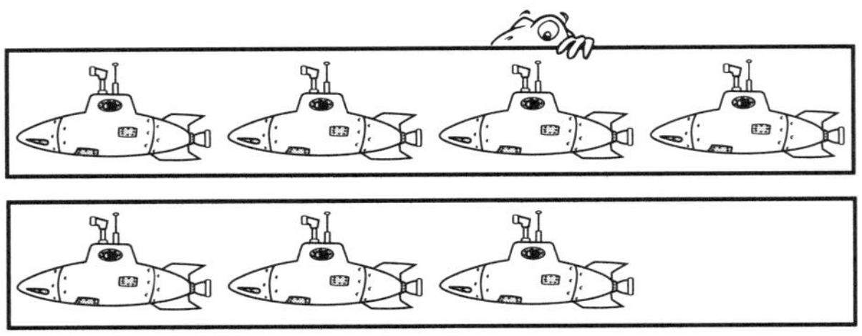

3 Eight fish, three swam away.

How many are left? ______

4 Finish this pattern.

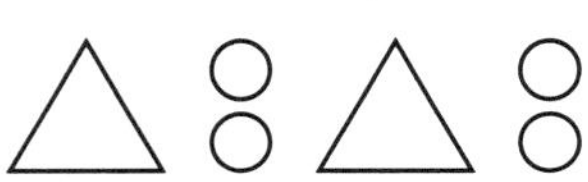 ______ ______

5

1st, ______, ______, 4th, ______

6 16, ______, 18, ______, 20

7

______ take away ______

is equal to ______.

8 Colour one half of each picture.

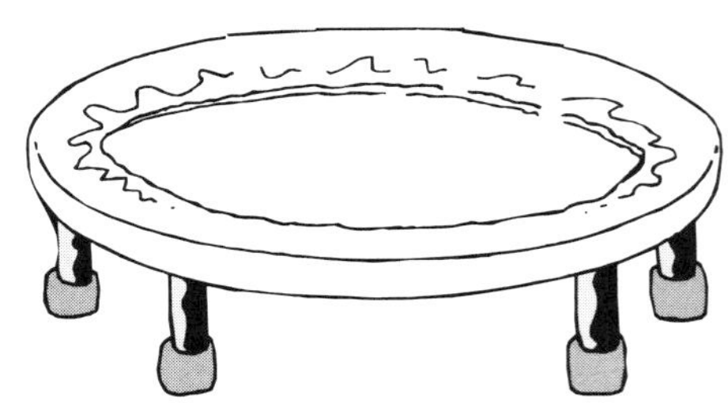

9 Cross out 18 hearts.

 • *AUSTRALIAN SIGNPOST MATHS 1 MENTALS* • ISBN 978 1 4886 2177 2

1:2

❶ Draw one cow **inside** the paddock.

Draw two birds **above** the tree.

Draw a dog **next to** the tree.

❷ Colour half of each shape.

❸ Colour 3 red and 2 blue.

_____ fish

1:3

❶ Complete each pattern.

How many birds? ☐

a  _____ _____ _____

b 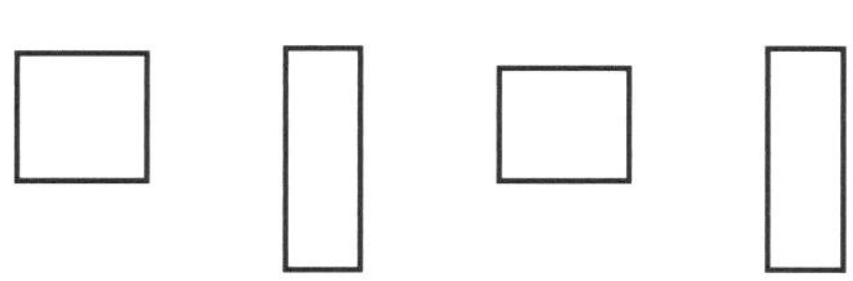 _____ _____ _____

c  _____ _____ _____

1. Trace and copy each word.

two ________

four ________

five ________

six ________

2. Colour the shapes that are divided into halves.

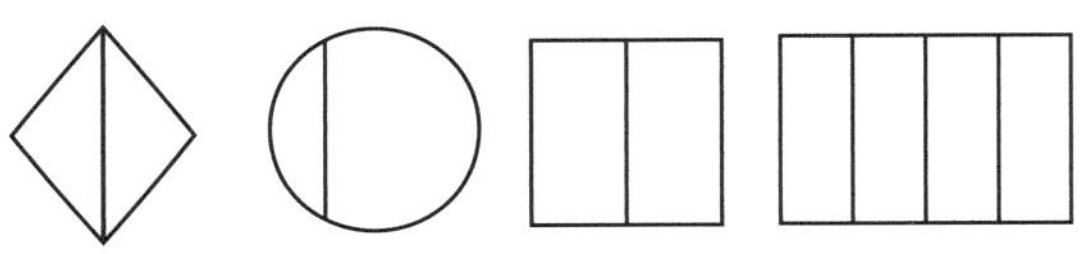

3. Circle the objects that are easy to lift.

4. Name this shape.

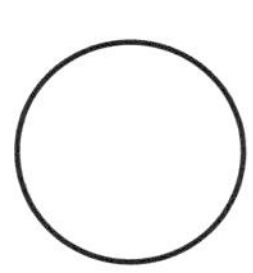

____

5. How many boats? ____

6. Write the missing numbers.

a 2, ___, 4, 5, ___, ___

b 10, 9, 8, 7, ___, ___, ___

7.

8 take away 2 equals ____.

8. Circle the one that holds the most.

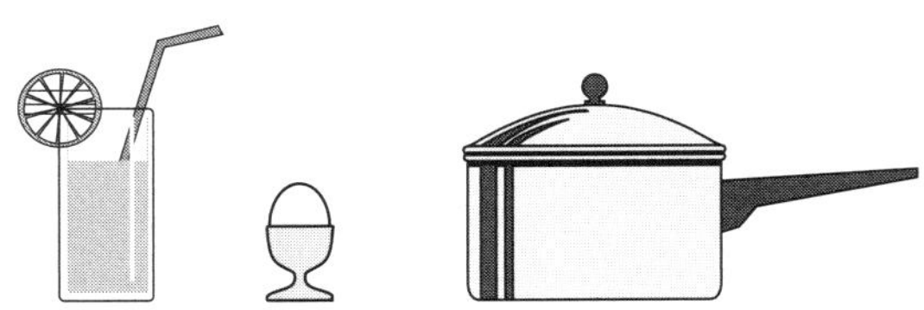

9. Draw a line to cut this pie in half.

 • *AUSTRALIAN SIGNPOST MATHS 1 MENTALS* • ISBN 978 1 4886 2177 2

2:2

❶ Colour 1 blue and 3 yellow.

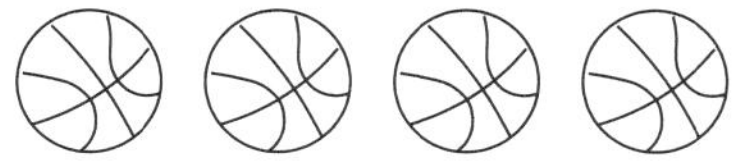

____ balls

❷ Match:

six *eight* *one* *ten* *two*

8 6 10 2 1

❸ Ten lollipops, five fell on the ground.

How many left? ____

2:3

1 2 3 4 5 6 7 8 9 10

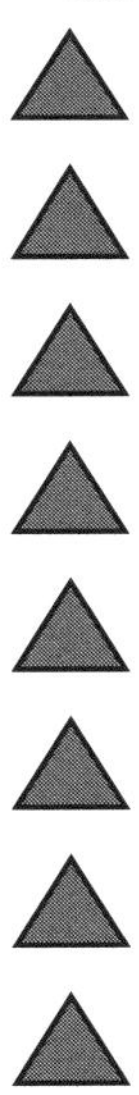

❶ Trace, then write each word.
Draw shapes to show each number.

one ____________

three ____________

seven ____________

eight ____________

❶ What number comes before 8?

____

❷ 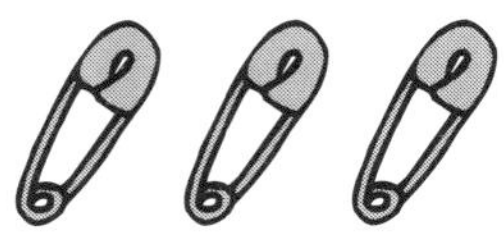 and 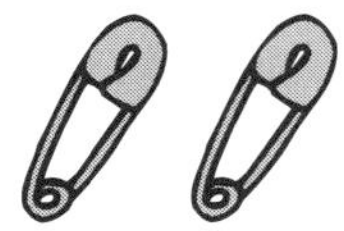

makes ____ pins.

❸ Circle the bird **above** the tree.

❹ Write the number twelve. ____

❺ Circle the heavy things.

❻ Colour one half of each.

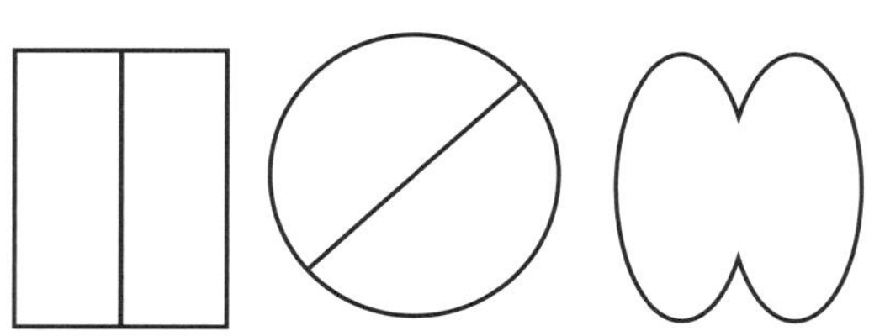

❼ The day after Monday.

____

❽ Write the missing numbers.

11, 12, ____, 14, ____, ____,

____, 18, ____, ____

❾ Write the numbers in order, from smallest to biggest.

a 4, 8, 2, 6

____, ____, ____, ____

b 7, 6, 8, 5

____, ____, ____, ____

❿ Draw 5 more lollipops.

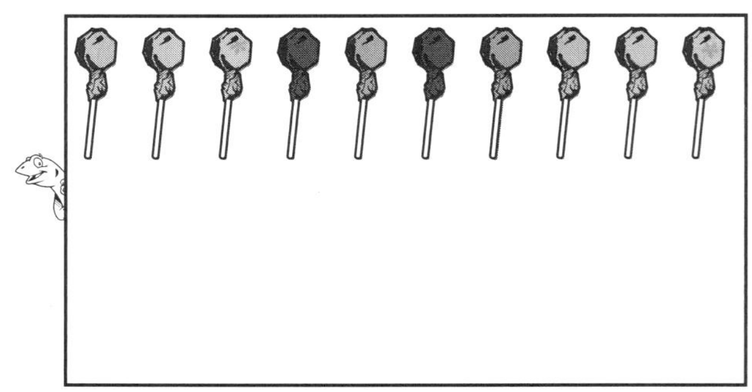

How many altogether? ____

⓫ Circle the one that can hold the most.

⓬ How many leaves? ____

 • *AUSTRALIAN SIGNPOST MATHS 1 MENTALS* • ISBN 978 1 4886 2177 2

3:2

❶ Write the missing numerals.

0, ___, ___, 3, ___, ___, 6, ___, ___, ___, ___

❷ Match each number with its name.

3 4 1 2 7 5 6 10 9 8

one two three four five six seven eight nine ten

❸ Count on by ones. 15, 16, ___, ___, ___, ___

❹ Count back by ones. 20, 19, ___, ___, ___, ___

❺ How many days in a week? ___

❻ Draw pictures to complete the problem.

3 circles and 6 circles makes ___ circles.

3:3

❶ Draw your own pictures.

3 and 4 makes ___.

4:1

 + 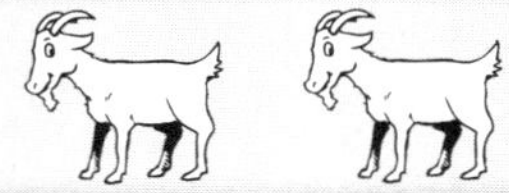 = ____

❶ Draw more balls to make 8.

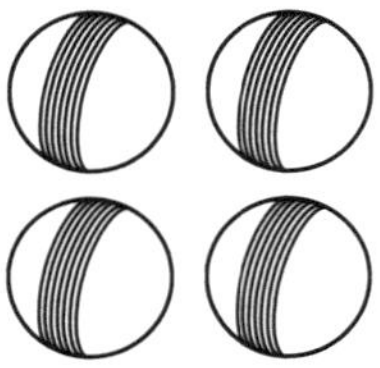

❷  and 

____ and ____ makes ____.

3 + 2 = ____

❸ Write the missing ordinal numbers.

1st, ____, 3rd, 4th, ____

❹ 10 take away 5 equals ____.

❺ Draw two squares.

❻ Count back by ones.

17, 16, ____, ____, ____

❼

____ birds

3 fly away.

____ birds left.

❽ The number after 16. ____

The number before 20. ____

❾ This clock shows

____ o'clock.

❿ Colour 3 milkshakes pink and 2 milkshakes yellow.

How many milkshakes are coloured? ____

 • *AUSTRALIAN SIGNPOST MATHS 1 MENTALS* • ISBN 978 1 4886 2177 2

4:2

1. Write the missing positions.

1st ______ ______ 4th ______

2. Count the shapes in this picture.

circles ______

triangles ______

rectangles ______

3. Write these numbers in order, starting with the smallest.

19, 17, 15, 13, 11

______, ______, ______, ______, ______

4:3

11 12 13 14 15 16 17 18 19 20

1. Count the coloured squares and complete.

a 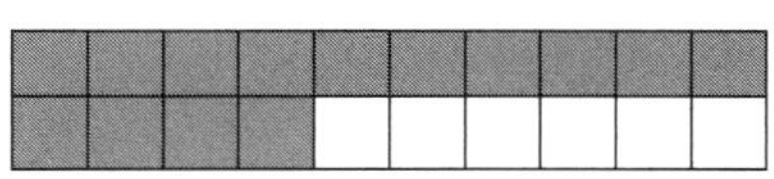

10 and 4 makes ______.

b 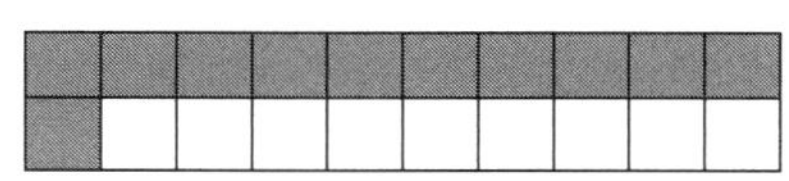

10 and 1 makes ______.

c 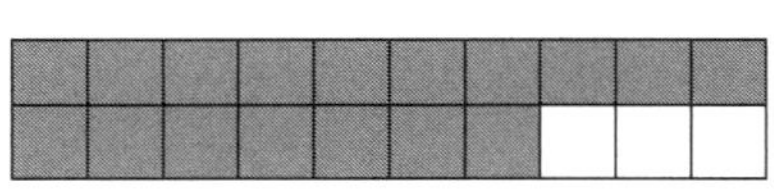

10 and 7 makes ______.

d 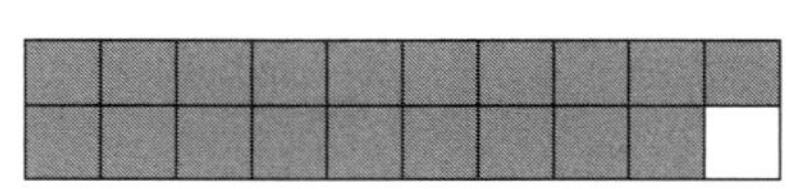

10 and 9 makes ______.

e 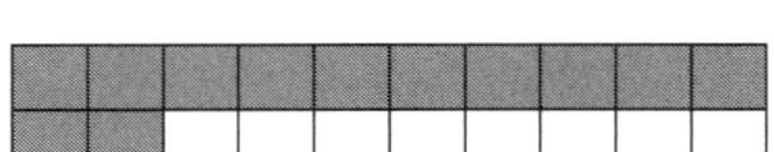

10 and 2 makes ______.

f 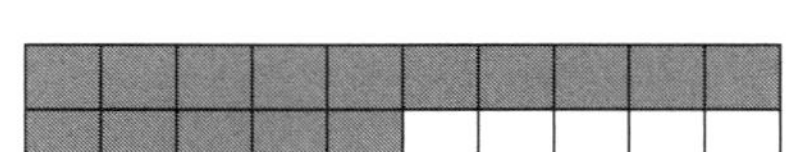

10 and 5 makes ______.

❶

 and 

____ + ____ = ____

❷ Draw 6 o'clock on the clock face.

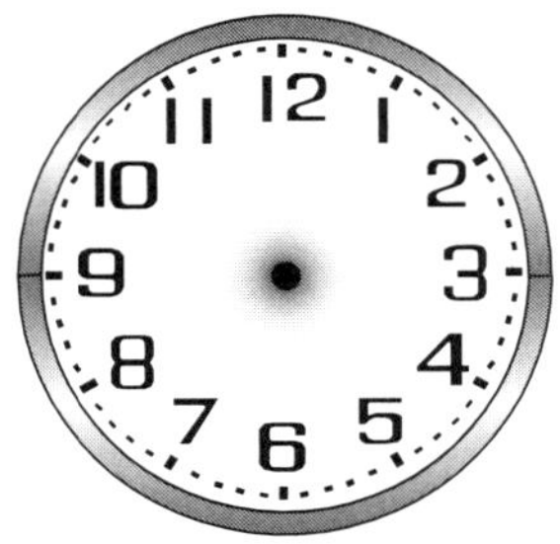

❸ Five owls.
Two flew away.

How many left? ____

❹

1st, ____, 3rd, 4th, ____

❺ Draw a triangle.

❻ Count by ones. 

16, ____, 18, ____, ____

❼ Colour to show 17.

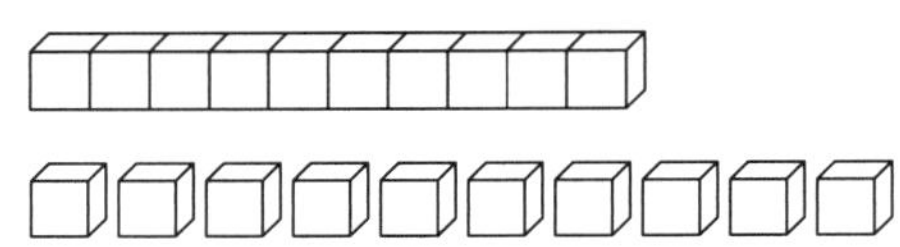

❽ Draw another object with straight edges.

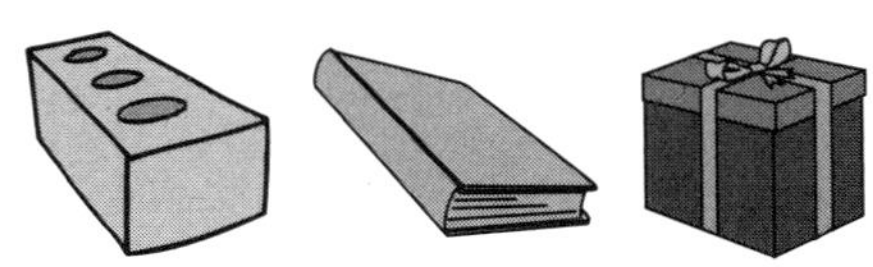

❾ 

Colour 4 green and 2 red.

____ leaves.

❿ What number follows?

12	

19	

 • *AUSTRALIAN SIGNPOST MATHS 1 MENTALS* • ISBN 978 1 4886 2177 2

5:2

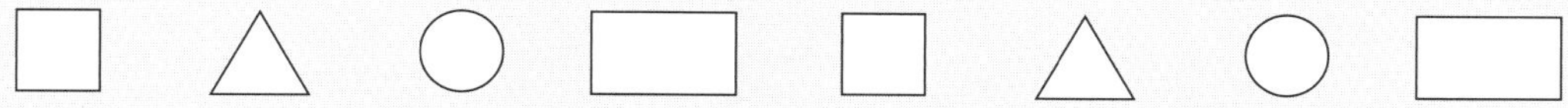

❶ Draw pictures to complete the problem.

4 squares and 4 squares makes ____ squares.

❷ Write the missing numbers.

		3				7		9	10
11					16			19	20

❸ Write these numbers in order, starting with the smallest.

12, 10, 13, 11

____, ____, ____, ____

5:3

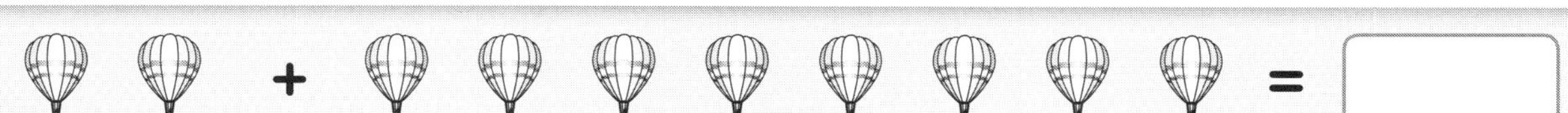

❶ Write the number shown.

a  ____

b 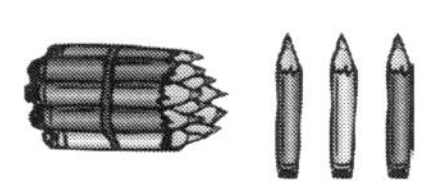 ____

c 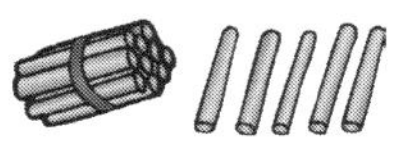 ____

d 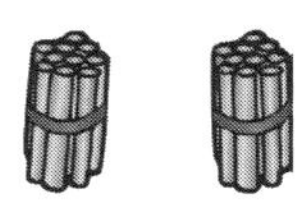 ____

e 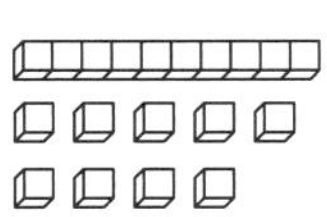 ____

f 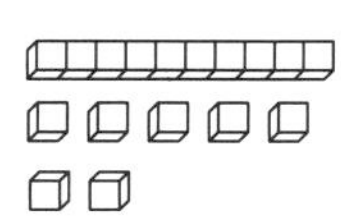 ____

❶ Eight bananas, three eaten. How many left? ____

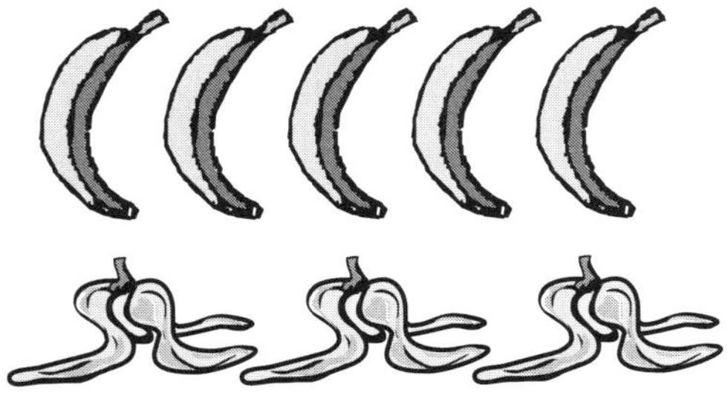

❷ Draw two rectangles.

❸ Count back by ones.

12, 11, 10, ____, ____, ____, ____, ____

❹ The number shown here is ____.

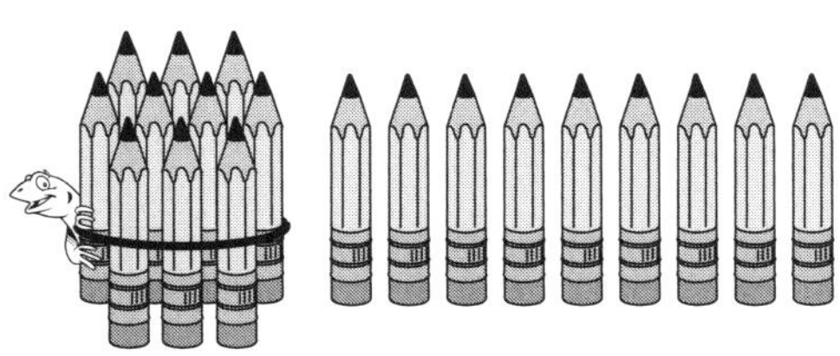

❺ Draw a line to cut each shape in half.

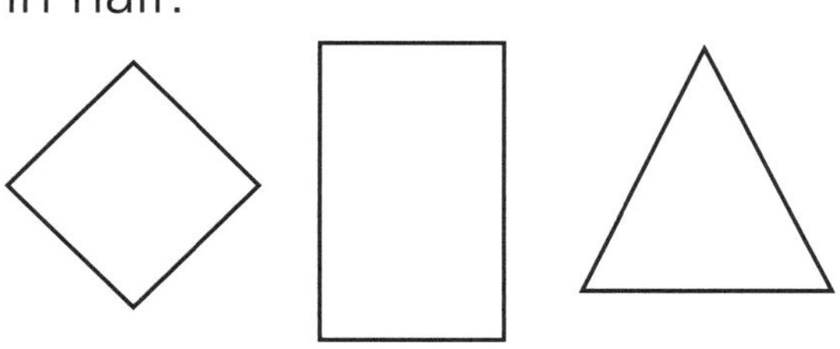

❻ Fill in the ordinal numbers.

2nd, ____, 4th, ____

❼ What shape is this?

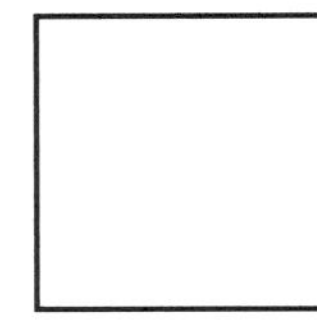

____

❽ Write the missing numbers.

	13	

	8	

❾ Match the shapes and objects.

❿ 10 and ____ makes ____.

10 + ____ = ____

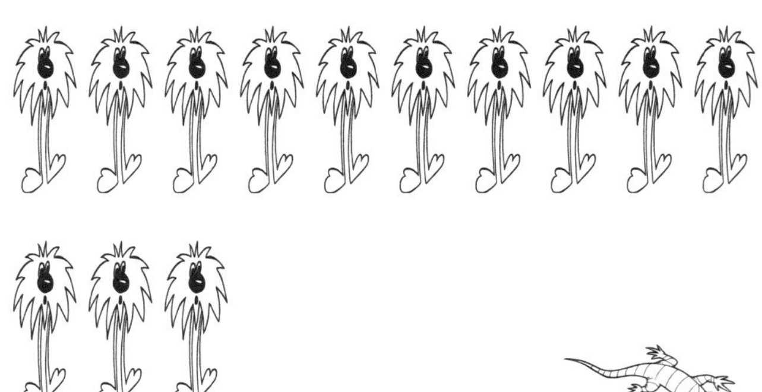

6:2

❶

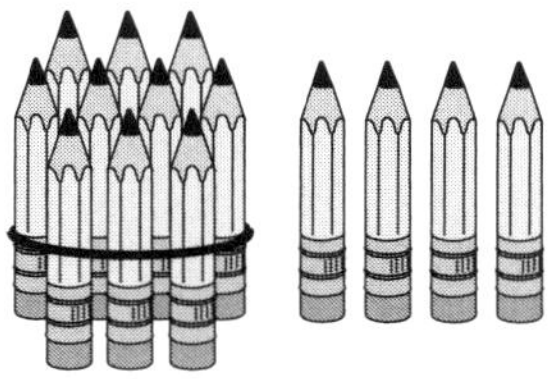

_____ and _____ = _____

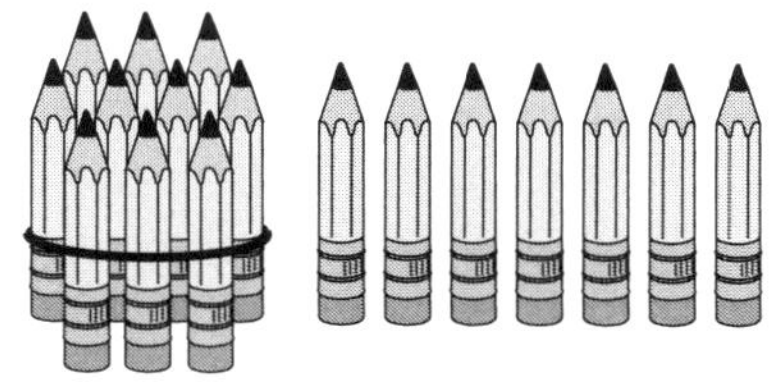

_____ and _____ = _____

❷ Write the number that comes before:

	7

	10

	17

	20

❸ Finish each number pattern.

a 3, 4, 5, 6, ____, ____, ____, ____

b 13, 14, 15, 16, ____, ____, ____, ____

c 23, 24, 25, 26, ____, ____, ____, ____

6:3

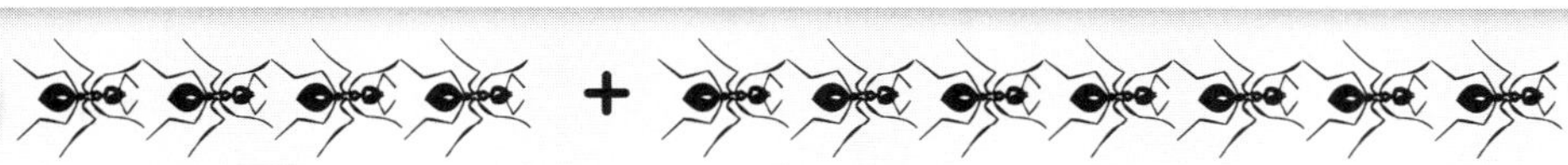

+ = [ ]

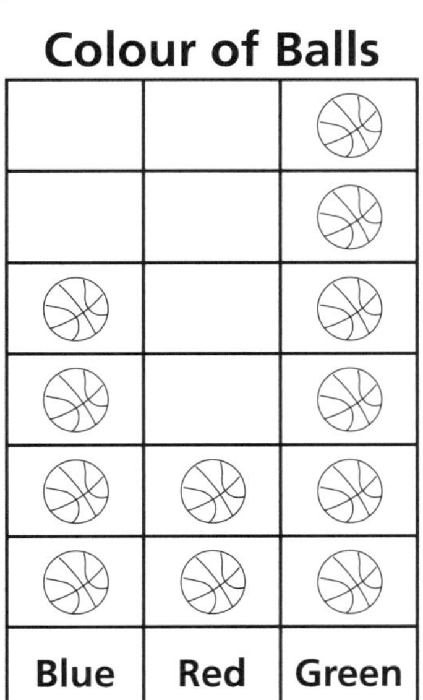

❶ Use this graph to answer the questions.

a How many balls are blue? _____

b How many balls are green? _____

c How many balls altogether? _____

d How many more blue balls than red balls? _____

e How many blue and red balls are there? _____

 • *AUSTRALIAN SIGNPOST MATHS 1 MENTALS* • ISBN 978 1 4886 2177 2

7:1

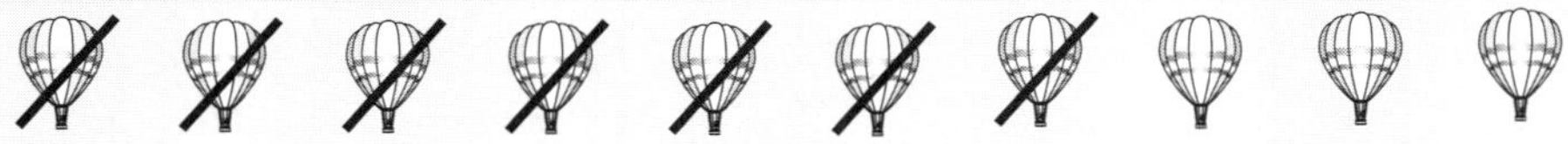

❶ Fill in the missing numbers.

14, ____, 16, ____, 18

❷ Match the shapes.

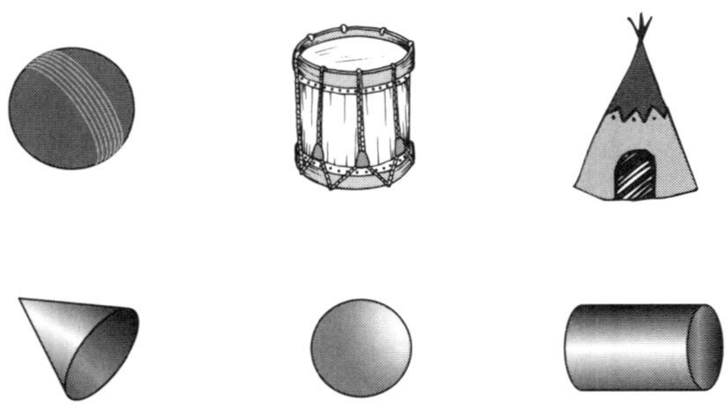

❸ Fill in the missing numbers.

____ + ____ = ____

❹ Colour the shapes that are divided into halves.

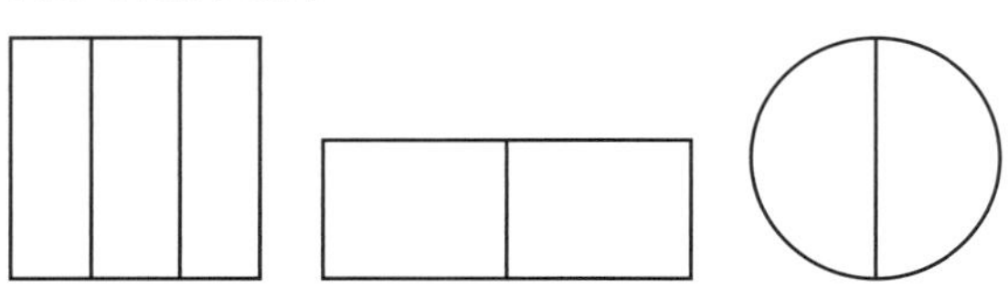

❺ Ten mules.

If three run away,
how many will be left? ____

❻ What is the time?

____ o'clock ____ o'clock

❼ **Animals We Saw**

a How many koalas? ____

b How many kangaroos? ____

c How many platypuses? ____

d Which column has the least animals? ____

e Which column has the most? ____

 • *AUSTRALIAN SIGNPOST MATHS 1 MENTALS* • ISBN 978 1 4886 2177 2

7:2

❶ Write a number pattern and rule to match the picture.

Add ☐ is the rule.

❷ Write the name of each number.

1	2	3
______	______	______
4	5	6
______	______	______

❸ Draw a line to halve each shape.

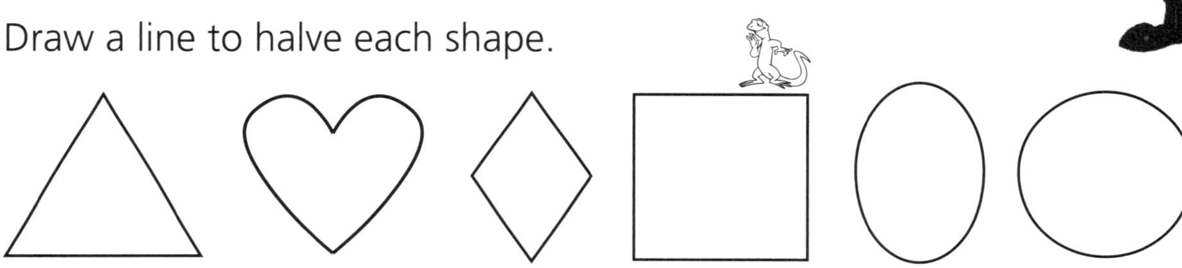

7:3

❶ Match these analogue and digital times.

How many? ☐

1

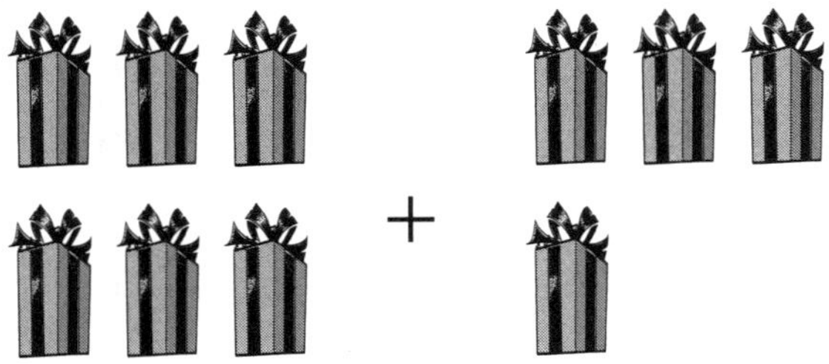

_____ + _____ = _____

2 What is the time?

_____ o'clock

3 What coin is this?

____

4 Join the dots to make a picture.

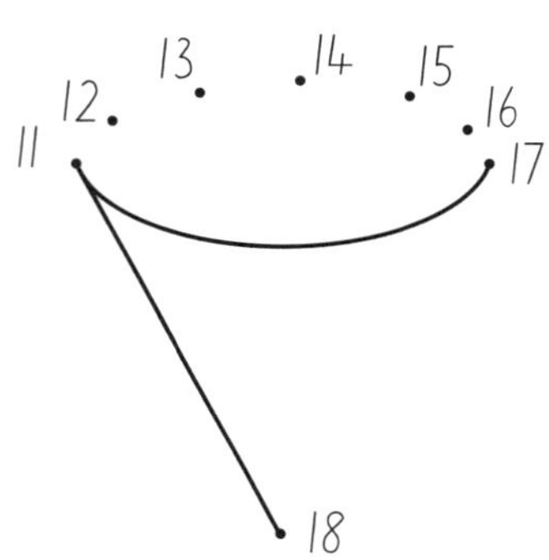

5 Name something longer than your arm.

____

6

_____ trees altogether

take away _____

is equal to _____.

7 Write the number sentence.

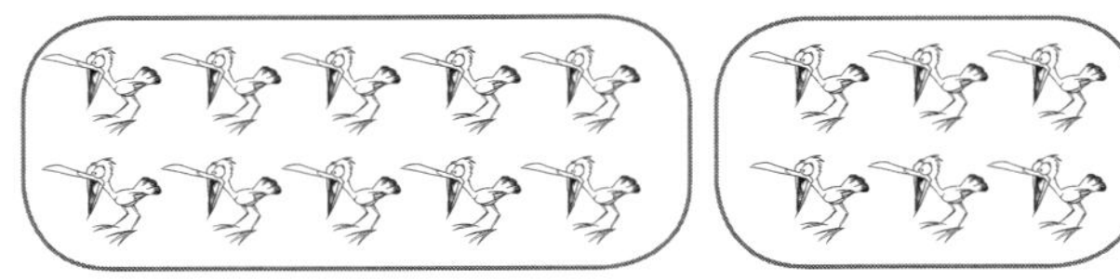

_____ + _____ = _____

8 What coin is this?

____

9

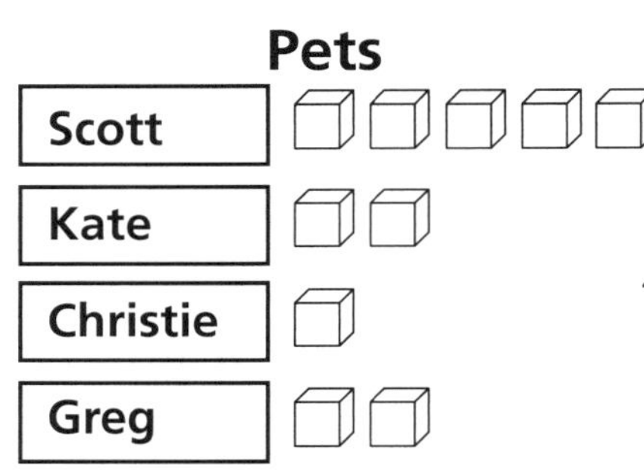

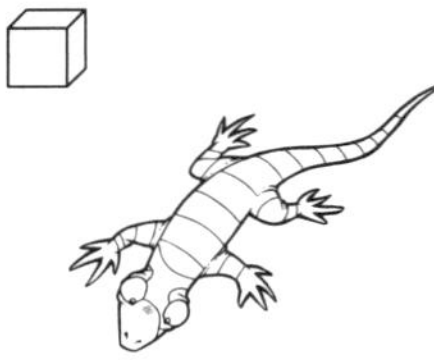

a How many pets altogether? __________

b Who has the most pets? __________

c Who has the least pets? __________

d How many more pets does Scott have than Kate? __________

 • *AUSTRALIAN SIGNPOST MATHS 1 MENTALS* • ISBN 978 1 4886 2177 2

8:2

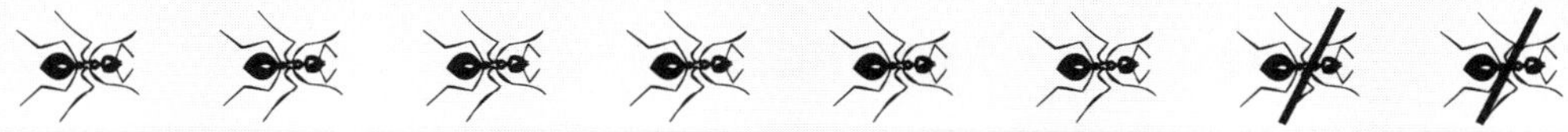

❶ Colour to match the shapes to the objects.

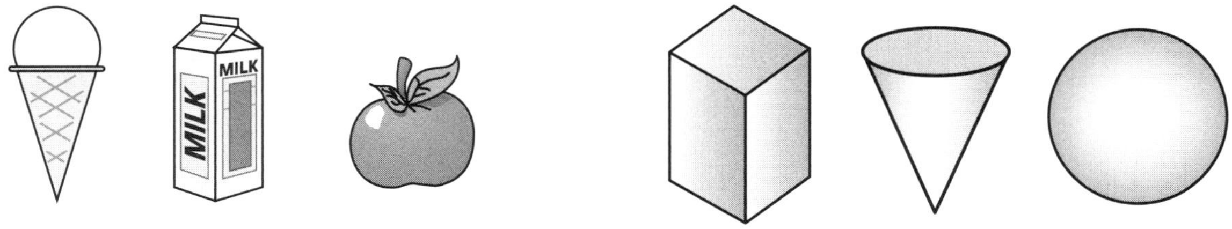

❷

a How many 5 cent coins? ______

b How many 10 cent coins? ______

c How many coins altogether? ______

d How many are not round? ______

8:3

double

❶ Use these pictures to answer the questions.

a

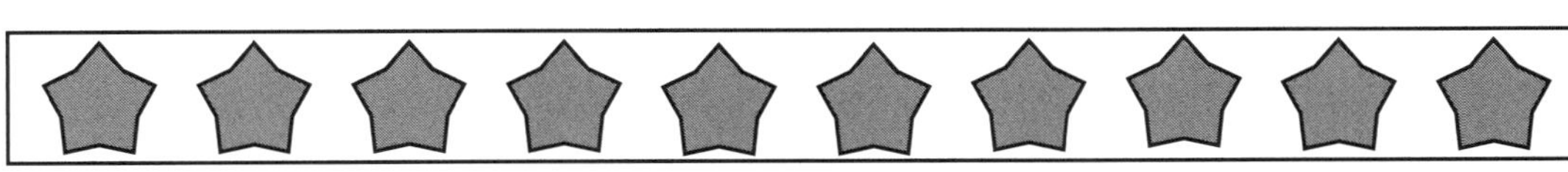

3 + 7 = ______ 9 + 1 = ______ 6 + 4 = ______ 2 + 8 = ______

5 + 5 = ______ 4 + 6 = ______ 10 + 0 = ______ 7 + 3 = ______

b

2 + 6 = ______ 1 + 7 = ______ 4 + 4 = ______ 5 + 3 = ______

8 + 0 = ______ 5 + 3 = ______ 6 + 2 = ______ 7 + 1 = ______

9:1 ☆ ☆ ☆ and ☆ ☆ makes ☆ ☆ ☆ ☆ ☆

1. What coin is this?

______

2. Double 3 is ______.

____ + ____ = ____

3. Complete:

a 14, ____, 16, ____, 18

b 2, ____, 20, ____, 18

4. Circle the light things.

5. Circle things longer than your ruler.

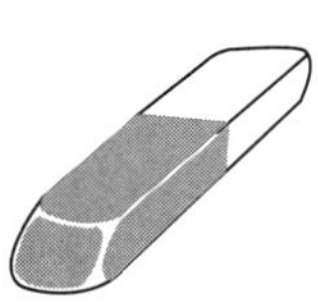

6. The pencil is ____ paperclips long.

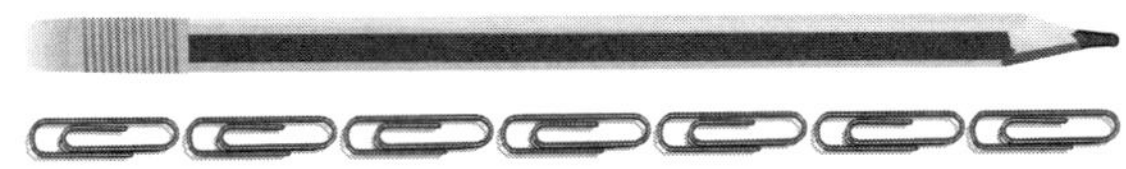

7. The day **after** Sunday.

______

8. Circle the group with the least.

9. The number **after** 23. ______

The number **before** 27. ______

10. Count by ones.

26, 27, ____, ____, ____

11. What coin is this?

______

12. 3 + 2 = ____ 6 + 4 = ____

8 + 3 = ____ 9 + 5 = ____

9:2

❶ Circle to match the sphere to an object.

❷ Match using coloured pencils. Use counters if you need help.

4 + 3	5	1 + 5
5 + 1	6	3 + 2
2 + 3	7	3 + 5
3 + 5	8	3 + 4

9:3

❶ **a** Double 4 = ______

______ + ______ = ______

b Double 5 = ______

______ + ______ = ______

c Double 6 = ______

______ + ______ = ______

d Double 8 = ______

______ + ______ = ______

e Double 2 = ______

______ + ______ = ______

f Double 7 = ______

______ + ______ = ______

10:1

❶ Join the dots to finish the shape.

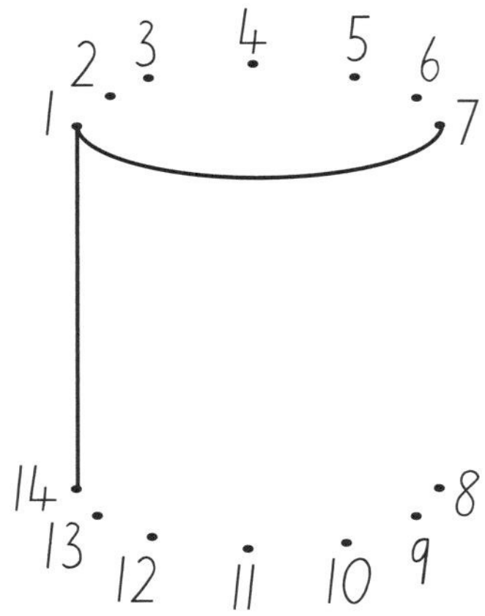

❷ Write the number sentence.

_____ + _____ = _____

❸ Circle the shortest person.

❹ How many erasers would be the same length as the pencil? _____

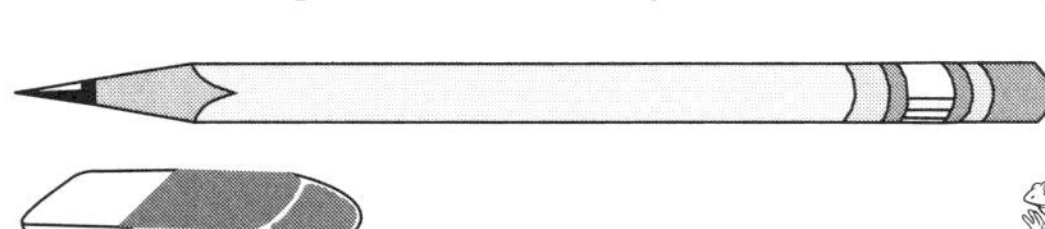

❺ Draw a longer tail.

❻ What coin is this?

____

❼ Draw an oval.

❽

There are ____ more circles than stars.

❾

Brick **Flowers**

The __________ is heavier than the __________.

❿ What coin is this?

____

 ISBN 978 1 4886 2177 2

10:2

☐ + ☐ = ☐

❶ Marco's cars ______ 

Yuri's cars ______ 

How many cars altogether? ______

How many more cars has Marco? ______ 9 – 4 = ______

❷ 0 + 5 = ___ 7 + 3 = ___ 6 + 3 = ___ 4 + 3 = ___

6 + 2 = ___ 5 + 5 = ___ 3 + 2 = ___ 2 + 8 = ___

❸ Circle the things that are lighter than the book.

10:3

double 3 = ☐

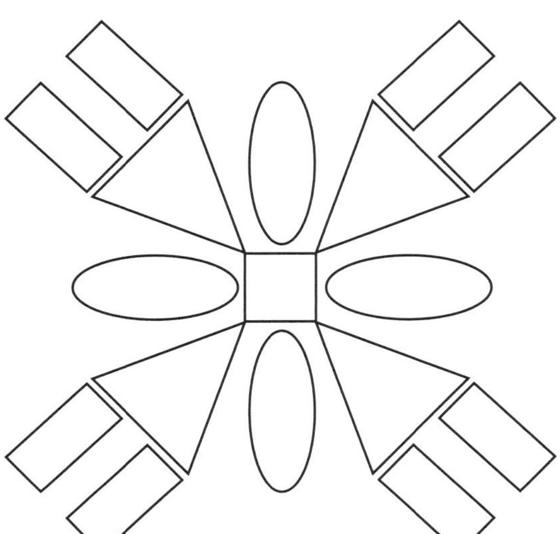

❶ How many:

a squares? ______

b rectangles? ______

c triangles? ______

d circles? ______

e ovals? ______

❷ Colour the design using the same colour for each shape.

11:1

1. How many balloons?

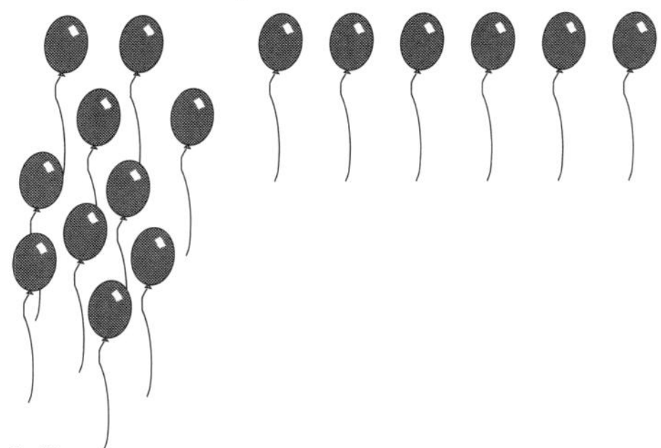

10 + ____ = ______

2. Finish the number pattern.

20, 30, 40, ______,

______

3. Draw a flag on the **left** flag pole.

4. Name something slower than a galloping horse.

____

5. Colour the longer pencil.

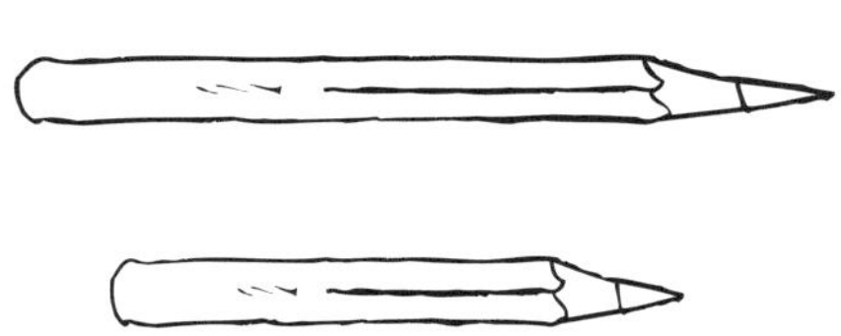

6. Which of our coins is worth the most?

____

7. 7 and 2 makes ______ .

8. Complete this pattern.

 ________

9.

Circle:

The brick is **lighter / heavier** than the book.

10.

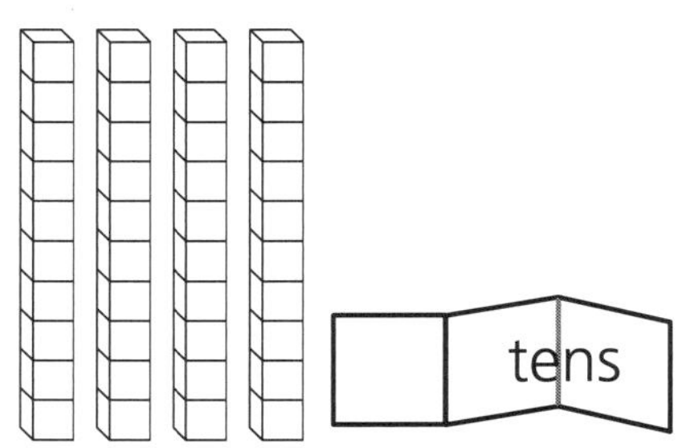

______

11. Colour the gold coins yellow.

11:2 10, 20, 30, 40, ____, ____, ____, ____

1

Lia has ____ flowers.

Bob has ____ flowers.

How many more has Lia than Bob? ________ 7 – 3 = ________

2 Circle groups of ten. How many triangles? ________

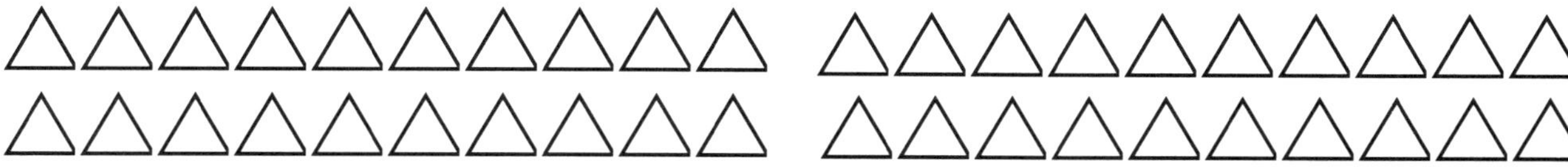

3 Complete.

5c	c	c	
five cents	cents	twenty	

11:3

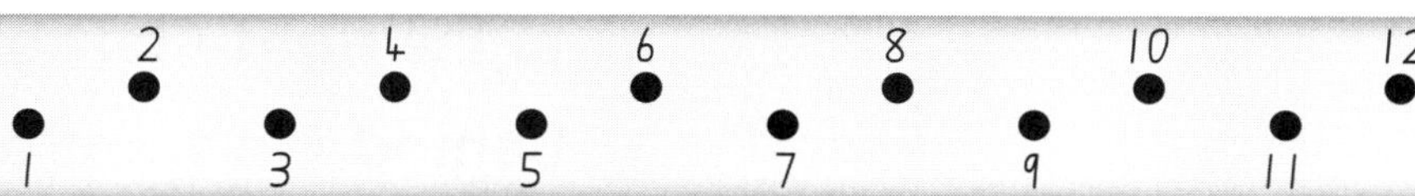

1 What is the number **after**:

19? ______ 40? ______

2 What is the number **before**:

13? ______ 37? ______

3 Complete the table.

1	2	3	4	5	6	7	8	9	10
11		13	14		16	17		19	
	22	23		25	26	27	28	29	30
31	32	33	34	35		37			40
	42		44	45	46		48	49	50

squares

1 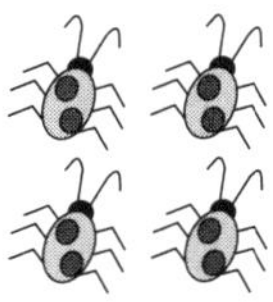 and 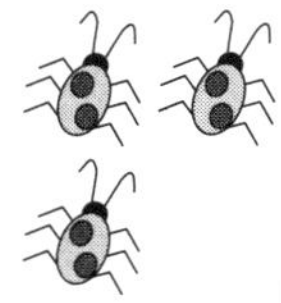

___ + ___ = ___

2 Continue the pattern.

 ______ ______

3 Finish the number pattern.

80, 70, 60, ______, ______

4 Finish the pattern.

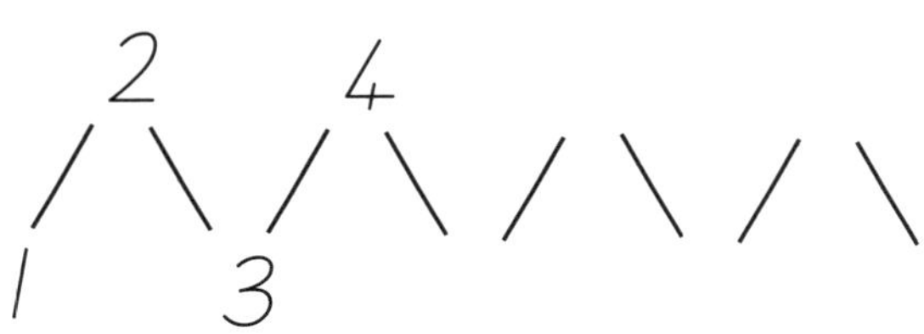

5 

6 take away 3 equals ______.

6 Write the numeral for:

- **a** four ______
- **b** seven ______
- **c** eleven ______
- **d** eighteen ______
- **e** eight ______

7 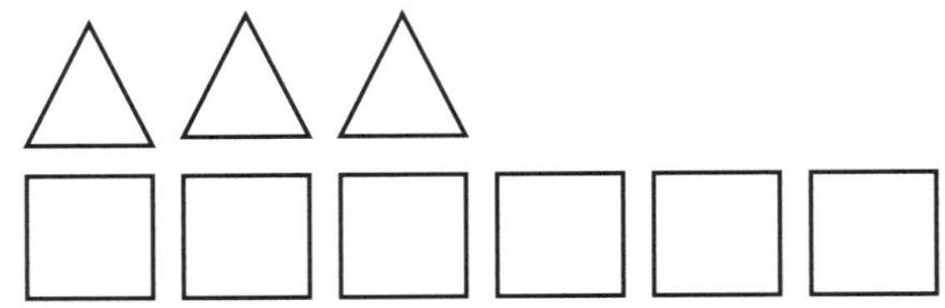

How many more squares are there? ______

6 − 3 = ______

8 

Circle.

The woman is:

to the **right / left** of the cashier,

behind / in front of the trolley.

9 3 + 4 = ______ 5 + 3 = ______

10 Number these bones in order of length, from shortest (1) to longest (3).

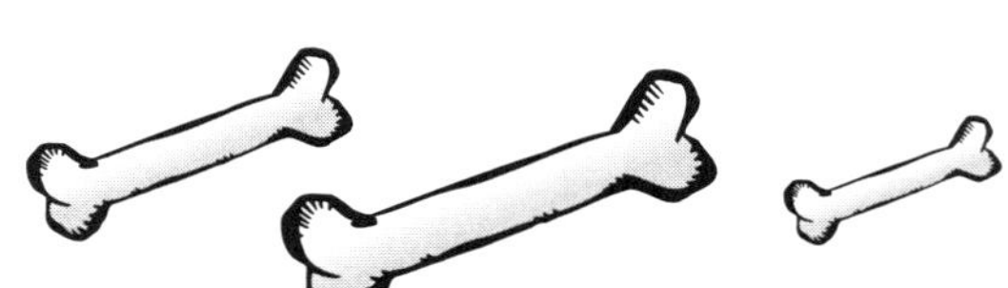

 • *AUSTRALIAN SIGNPOST MATHS 1 MENTALS* • ISBN 978 1 4886 2177 2

12:2

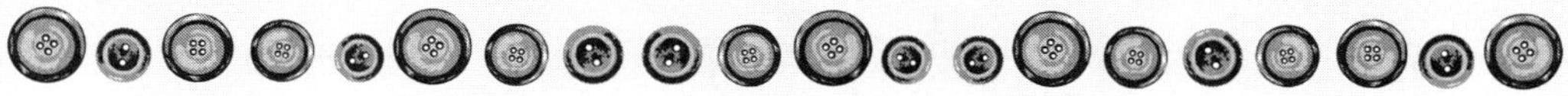

❶ Circle 3 tens.

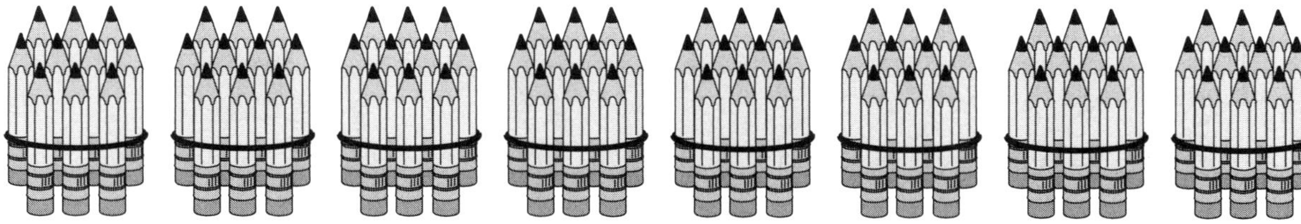

❷ Colour the coin with the greatest value red and the coin with the least value blue.

❸ Draw a tree on the **left** of the car
and a flower on the **right** of the car.

❹ 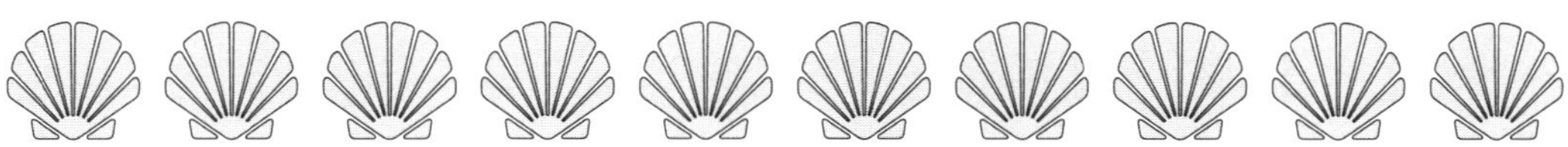

10 – 5 = ____ 10 – 4 = ____ 10 – 6 = ____ 10 – 3 = ____

12:3

❶ Draw 2 squares, 3 circles, 1 rectangle and 1 triangle.

13:1

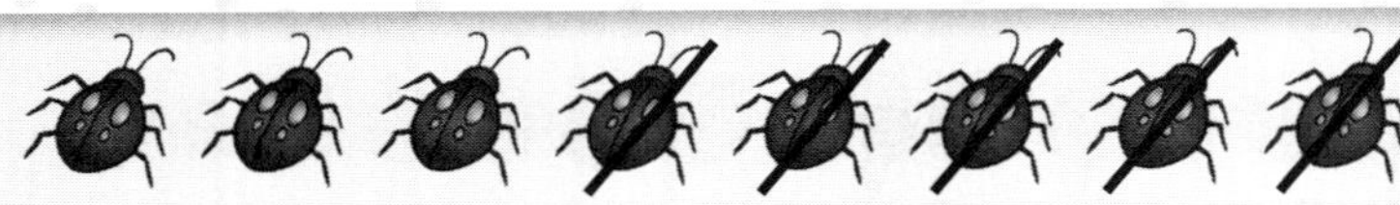

8 – 5 = ______

❶ 

10 – 4 = ____ 

❷ Finish these number patterns.

a 10, 20, 30, ____, ____, ____

b 90, 80, 70, ____, ____, ____,

____, ____

❸ 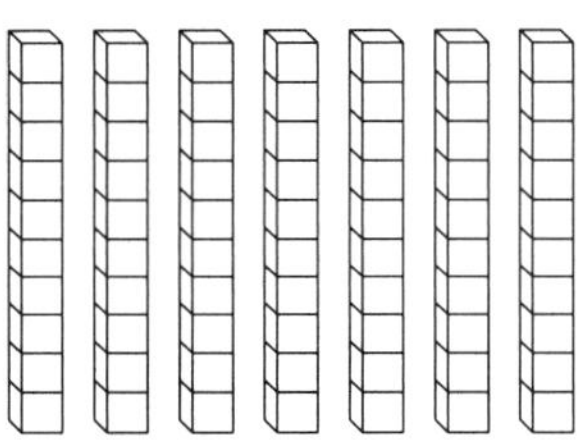 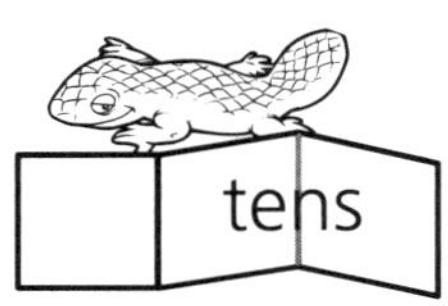

______

❹ Write the numeral for:

a fifteen ______

b ten ______

c twelve ______

d three ______

e nineteen ______

❺ Write the numerals in order, from 11 down to 7.

____, ____, ____, ____, ____

❻ 

Circle: The girl is on the **left / right** of the pony.

❼ Write the numeral for:

a eighty ______

b twenty ______

c sixty ______

❽ 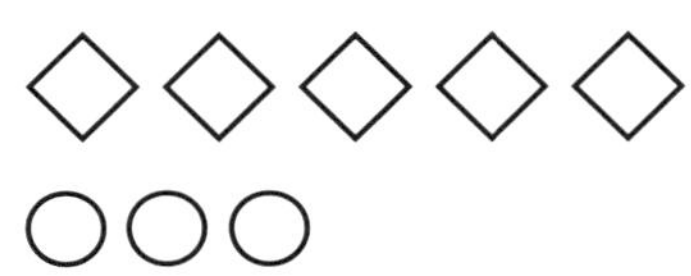

How many more squares are there? ______

5 – 3 = ______

❾ What shapes are used to make this pattern?

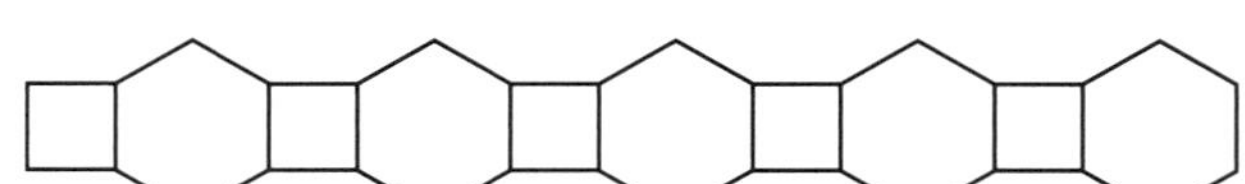

__________ and __________

❿ The day after Wednesday is

______________________________.

 ISBN 978 1 4886 2177 2

13:2

❶ a In the **bottom right-hand** corner of the box, draw a circle.

b At the **bottom on the other side**, draw a triangle.

c Draw two straight lines from the circle to the **top** of the box.

d Draw a car **below** the sun.

e Draw a boy **in the middle of** the box.

❷ a 20, 19, 18, ____, ____, ____, ____, ____, ____, ____, ____

b 6, 7, 8, ____, ____, ____, ____, ____, ____, ____, ____

13:3

❶ What is the number **after**:

26? ______ 49? ______

❷ What is the number **before**:

32? ______ 21? ______

❸ Complete the table.

1	2	3	4	5		7	8	9	10
11	12	13		15		17	18	19	
		23	24		26		28	29	30
	32		34	35	36	37	38	39	40
41	42	43	44		46	47		49	

14:1

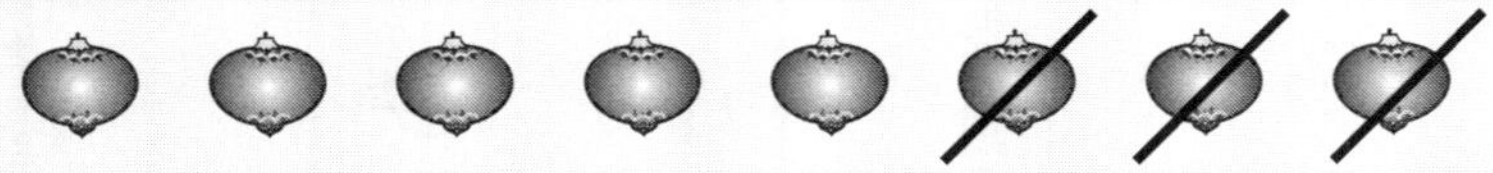

□ – □ = □

❶ Count on to find how many altogether.

7 + 2 = ___ 9 + 3 = ___

8 + 4 = ___ 5 + 2 = ___

❷ Tom has recess at ___ o'clock.

[:]

❸ Circle the objects that will roll down a hill.

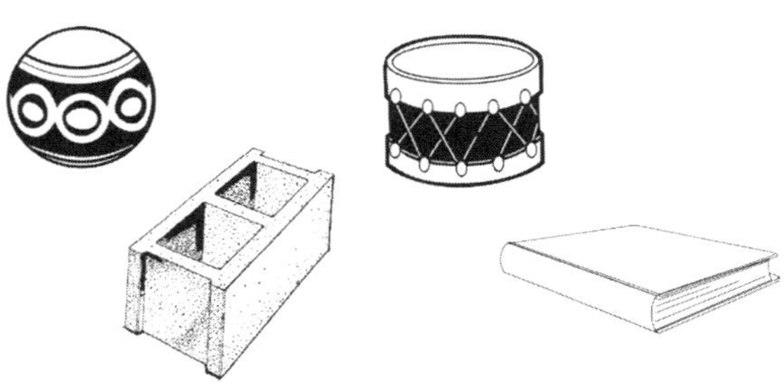

❹ Name the shapes used.

_____________ and _____________

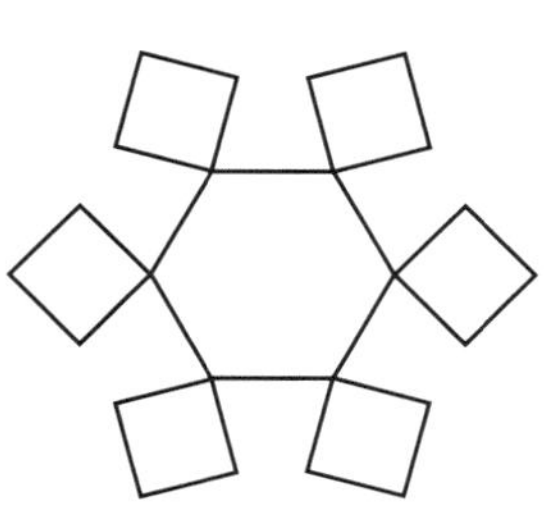

❺ Finish the pattern.

10, 20, 30, ___, ___, ___

❻ Join the dots counting by twos.

❼ Circle the objects that roll.

❽ Write the word for:

a 2 ____________

b 4 ____________

c 6 ____________

d 9 ____________

e 10 ____________

❾ 3 + 2 = ______

14:2

❶ How many tens altogether? ____ tens   Circle 7 tens.

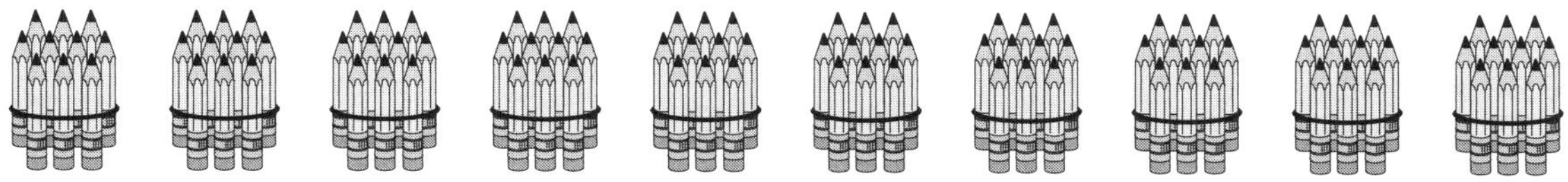

❷ Match the names and numerals.

80   30   50   90   60   40   70

fifty   thirty   eighty   ninety   sixty   seventy   forty

❸ Today is ______________.   Yesterday was ______________.

Tomorrow will be ______________.

❹ Put a circle in the **middle** triangle of each row.

Put a cross in the **bottom left** triangle.

Put a tick in the **bottom right** triangle.

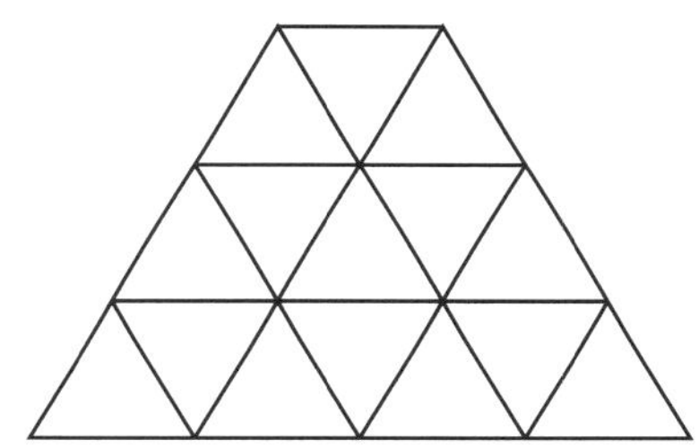

14:3

☐ + ☐ = ☐

❶ **a** Start at [4] count on [●●●] I get to [ ]

b [13] + [●●] = [ ]

c [15] + [●] = [ ]

d [6] + [●●●●] = [ ]

☐   ☐

☐

 • *AUSTRALIAN SIGNPOST MATHS 1 MENTALS* • ISBN 978 1 4886 2177 2

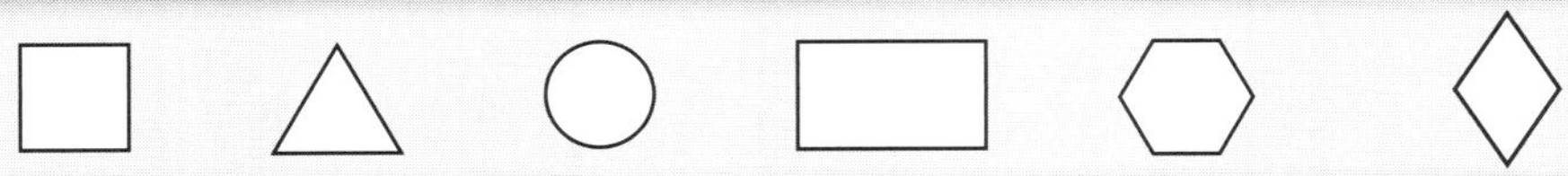

❶ Use counters to find the answers by counting on.

4 + 3 = ____ 6 + 5 = ____

5 + 2 = ____ 7 + 3 = ____

❷ 6:00 ________ o'clock

11:00 ________ o'clock

❸ ____ tens ____ ones = ____

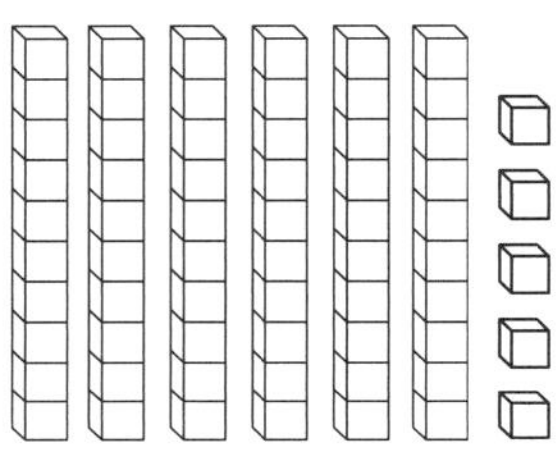

❹ Count back from:

a 7, ______, ______, ______

b 12, ______, ______, ______

c 18, ______, ______, ______

❺ **a** Continue this pattern.

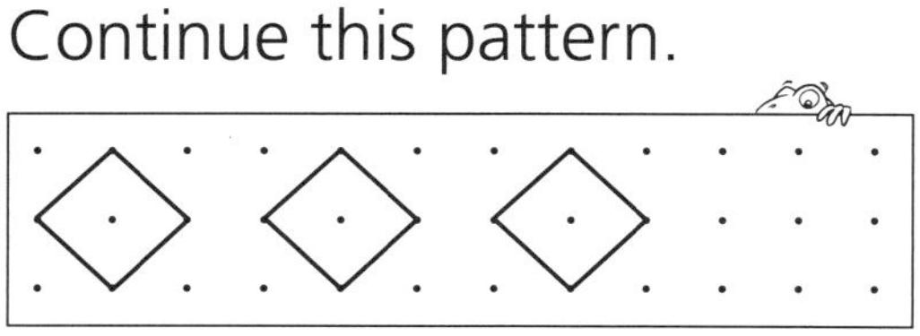

b What shape has been used?

____

❻ Name this shape.

____

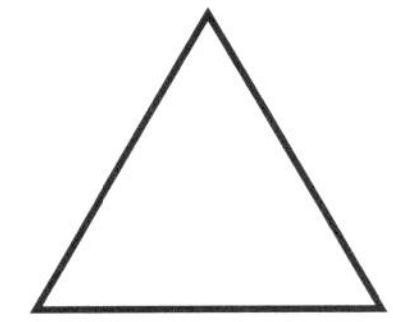

❼

= ______

❽ Circle the shape that does not belong.

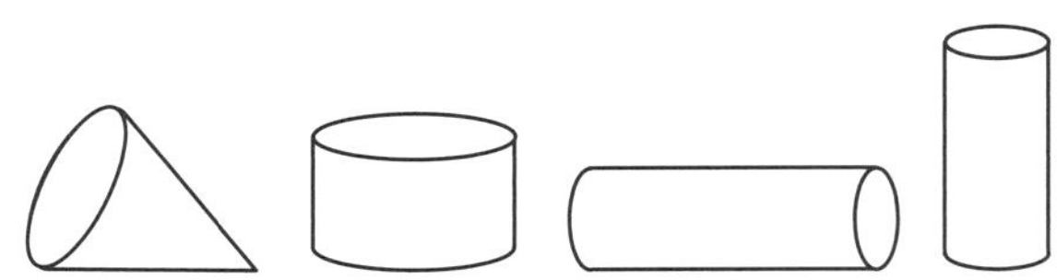

❾

______ + ______ = ______

Double 5 = ______

❿ Guess how many.

Guess = ______

Number = ______

 • *AUSTRALIAN SIGNPOST MATHS 1 MENTALS* • ISBN 978 1 4886 2177 2

15:2

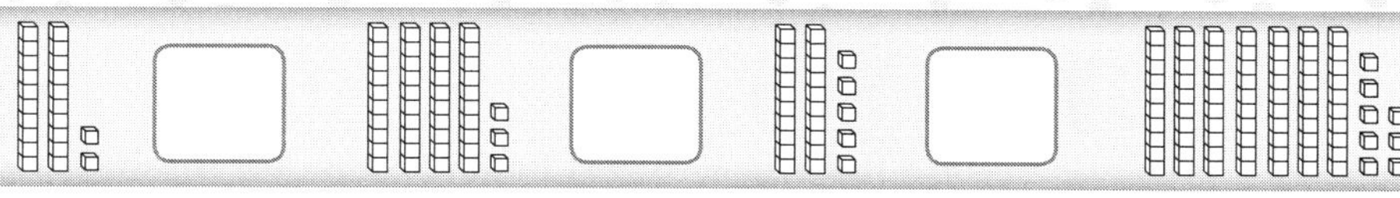

❶ Circle two objects that have the same shape.

❷ Tom has ____ cars.

Madeline has ____ cars.

How many more cars has Tom? ____

❸ Complete the numeral expander and write the whole number.

	te ns		on es

______

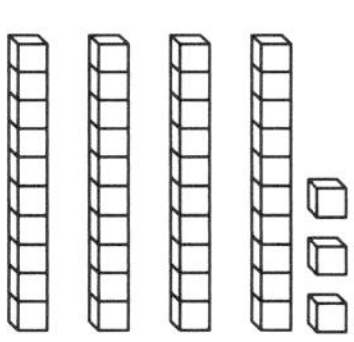

	te ns		on es

______

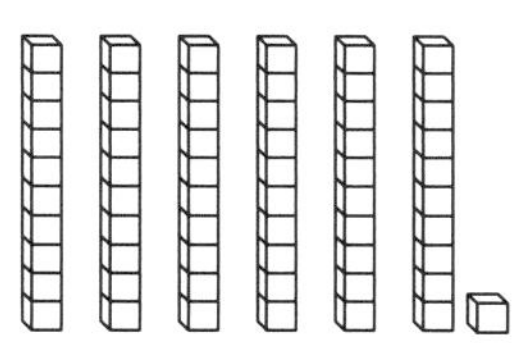

	te ns		on es

______

15:3

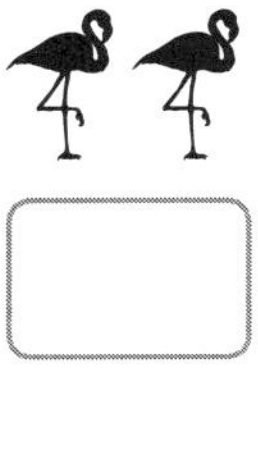

❶ Complete these number cards.

Tens	Ones
1	2

Tens	Ones

Tens	Ones

❶ Count back from:

a 9, ____, ____, ____

b 14, ____, ____, ____

c 20, ____, ____, ____

❷ Estimate how many cups would fill the carton.

____ cups

❸

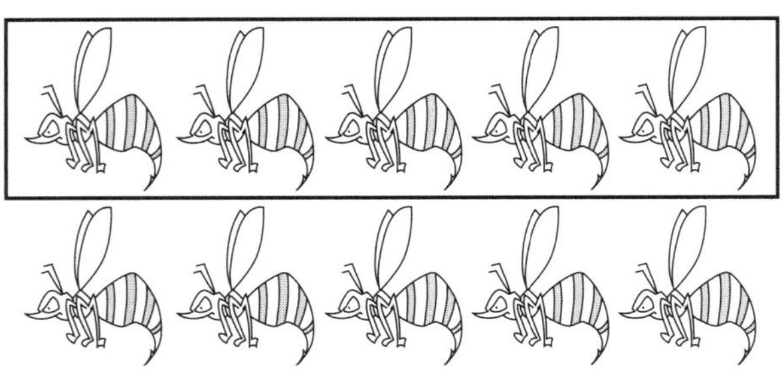

____ and ____ make ____.

❹

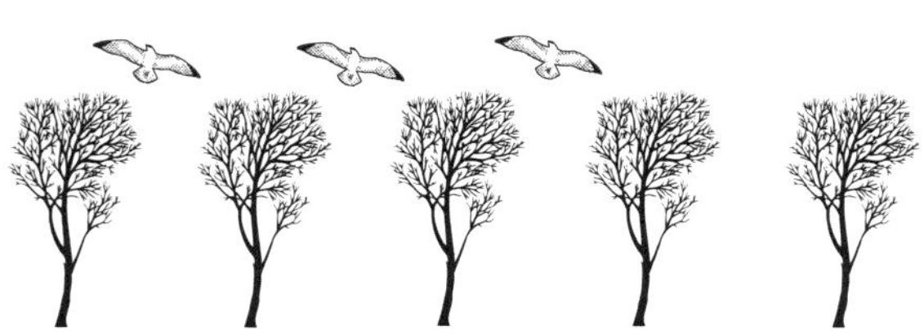

a How many birds? ____

b How many trees? ____

c How many more trees than birds? ____

d $5 - 3 =$ ____

❺ $5 + 8 =$ ____ $4 + 7 =$ ____

❻ Draw a rectangle and a triangle.

❼ Tick the bucket that would take the longest time to fill.

❽ Write the number sentence.

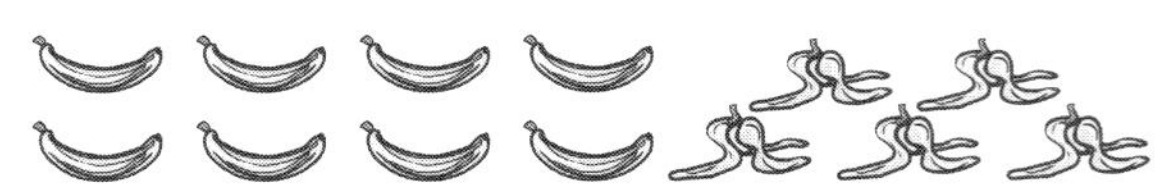

____ − ____ = ____

❾ Circle the heaviest object.

❿ This is a hexagon.

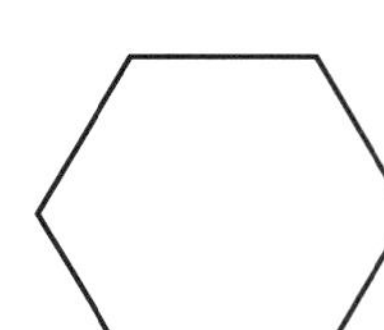

It has ____ sides.

It has ____ corners.

 • *AUSTRALIAN SIGNPOST MATHS 1 MENTALS* • ISBN 978 1 4886 2177 2

16:2

❶ Complete the numeral expander and write the whole number.

a 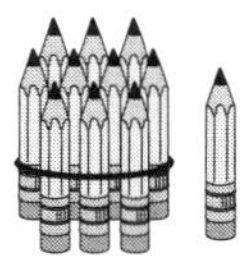

tens ones

______

b 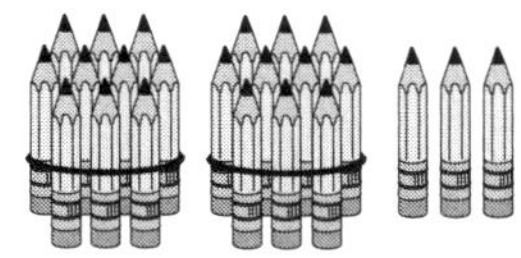

tens ones

______

c 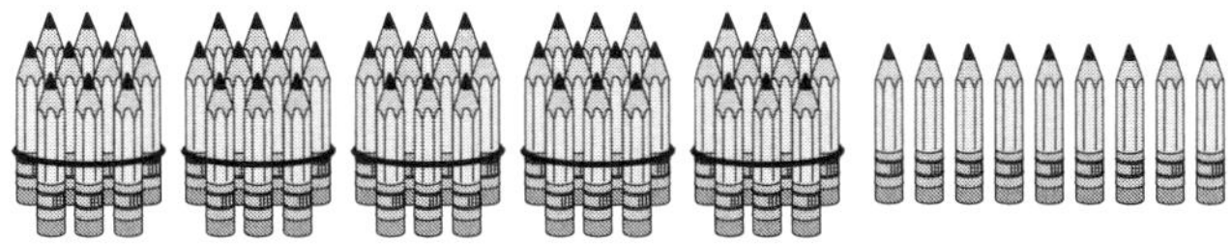

tens ones

______

d 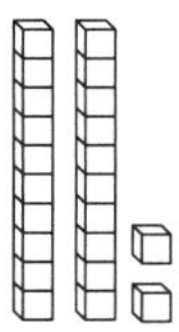

tens ones

______

e 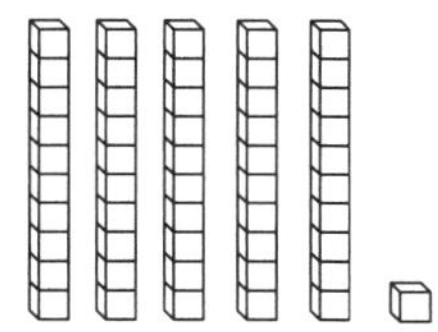

tens ones

______

f 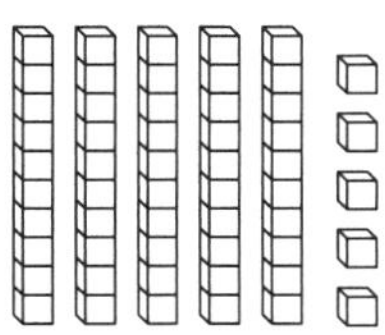

tens ones

______

g 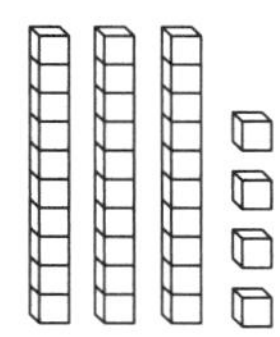

tens ones

______

❷ Fill in the missing numbers. Circle the numbers 10, 12, 14, 16 ,18 and 20.

10 11 12 13 14 ____ ____ ____ ____ ____ 20

16:3

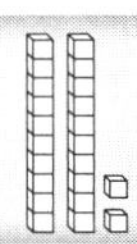 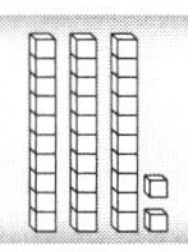 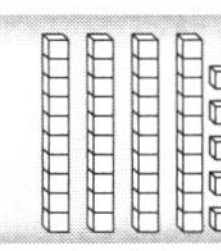

❶ The pencils are in bundles of 10.

How many in each group?

a 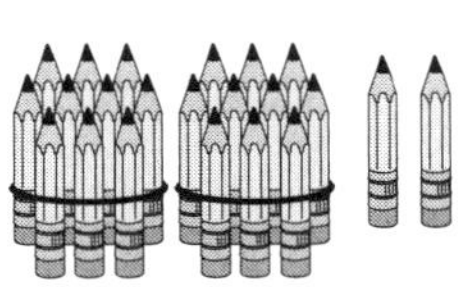 ______

b 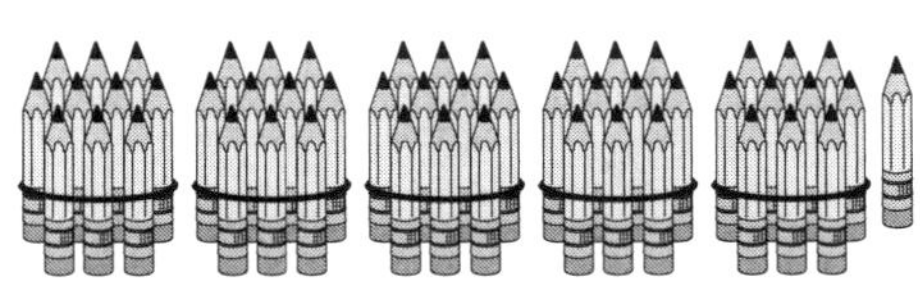 ______

c 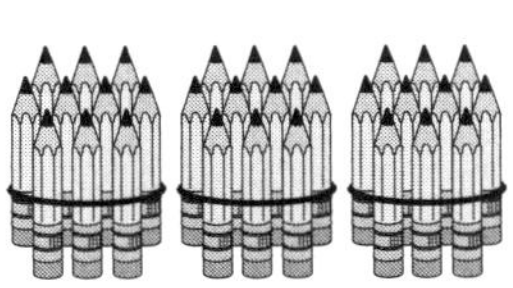 ______

d 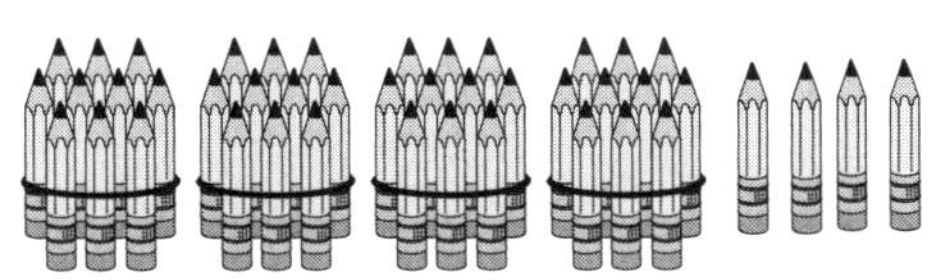 ______

1. How many days in 1 week? ____

2. Write these numbers in order.

7, 3, 9, 6

____, ____, ____, ____

3. Finish the number pattern.

8, 10, 12, ____, ____

4. 5 + 3 = ____

5. **a** Fill in the numbers.

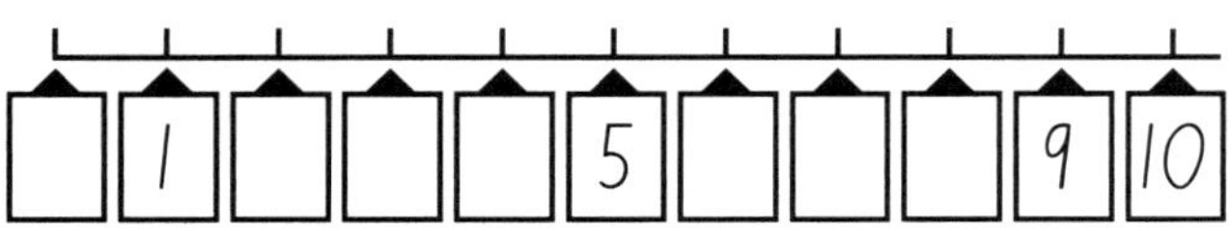

b Colour the numbers 2, 5 and 7 on this number line.

6. Estimate, then count the number of marbles.

Estimate = ________

Number = ________

7. Complete: I will probably eat

____________________ tonight.

8. How many dots?

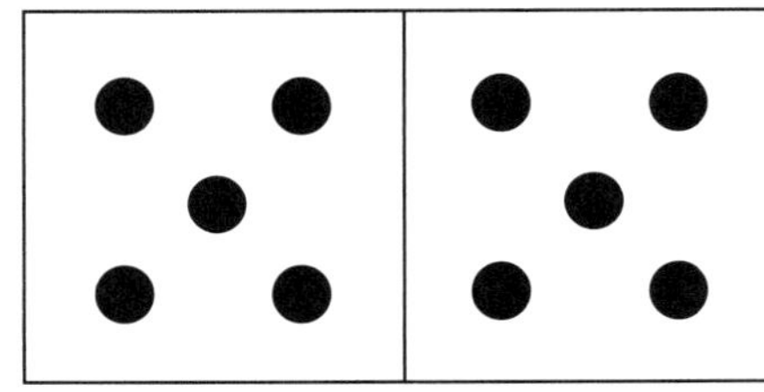

____ + ____ = ______

9. Draw a square.

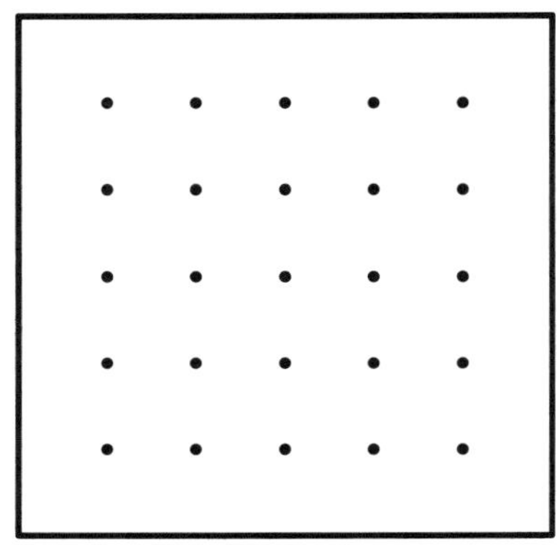

10. Estimate how many eggcups would fill the teacup.

____ eggcups.

11. Write the numeral for:

a twelve ____________

b fifteen ____________

c eighteen ____________

d seventeen ____________

 • *AUSTRALIAN SIGNPOST MATHS 1 MENTALS* • ISBN 978 1 4886 2177 2

Answers

Answers ID Card A

1 addition **2** subtraction **3** is equal to **4** number line
5 ordinal numbers **6** numeral expander **7** abacus
8 ones (place-value) block **9** tens (place-value) block
10 hundreds (place-value) block **11** half (of a whole)
12 half (of a collection) **13** dollar sign **14** cents sign
15 5 cent coin **16** 10 cent coin **17** 20 cent coin
18 50 cent coin **19** $1 coin **20** $2 coin **21** $5 note
22 $10 note **23** $20 note **24** $50 note
25 $100 note **26** hand span **27** equal arm balance
28 digital time **29** o'clock **30** half past

Answers ID Card B

1 circle **2** oval **3** triangle **4** square **5** rectangle
6 rhombus **7** hexagon **8** straight line **9** curved line
10 zigzag line **11** broken line **12** cube (box-shaped object) **13** sphere (ball-shaped object) **14** cylinder (can-shaped object) **15** cone (cone-shaped object)
16 left hand **17** right hand **18** above **19** below
20 forwards **21** backwards **22** full **23** half full
24 empty **25** longer **26** shorter **27** taller
28 heavy **29** light **30** picture graph

1:1

7 (tomatoes)

❶ 4 ❷ 7 ❸ 5 ❹ 

❺ 1st, 2nd, 3rd, 4th, 5th ❻ 16, 17, 18, 19, 20

❼ 8 take away 3 is equal to 5.

❽ Half of each will be coloured. 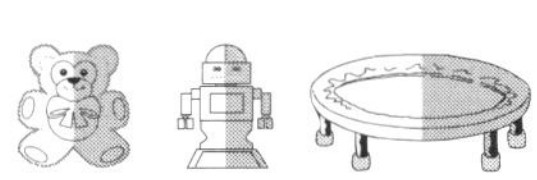

❾  Two will not be crossed out. Answers will vary.

1:2

9 (beetles)

❶ The circled animals will be drawn.

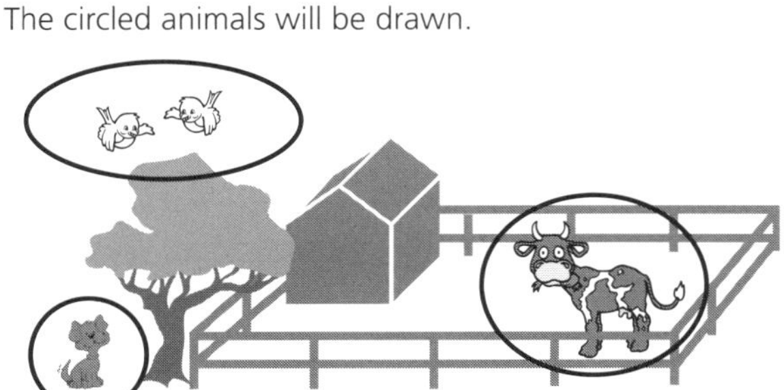

❷ 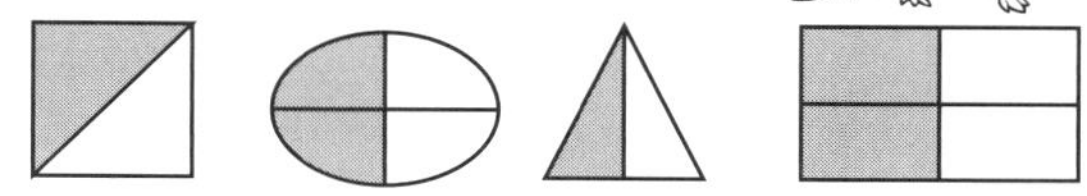

❸ 5 fish: 3 fish will be coloured red and 2 will be blue.

1:3

10 (strawberries)

❶ 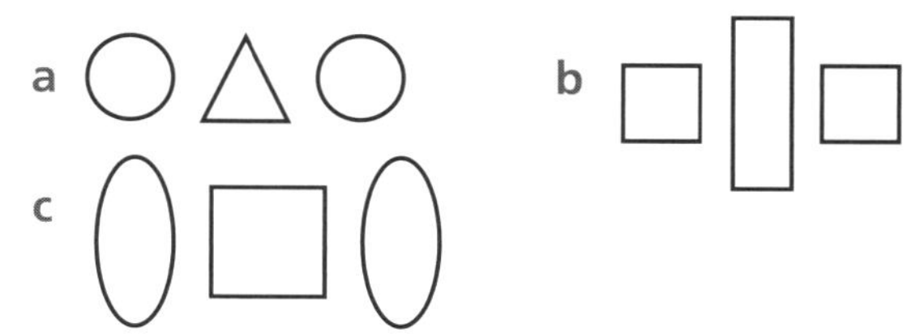

30 birds

2:1

6 (scooters)

❶ Each word will be traced and copied.

❷ 

❸ 

❹ circle ❺ 14 boats

❻ **a** 2, 3, 4, 5, 6, 7 **b** 10, 9, 8, 7, 6, 5, 4

❼ 6 ❽ 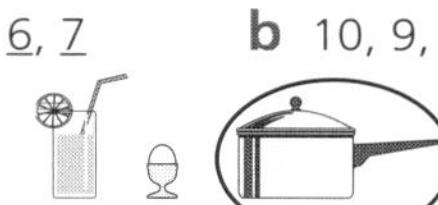 ❾ 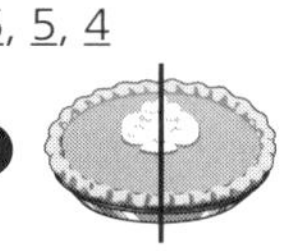

2:2

10 (horses)

❶ 1 ball will be coloured blue and 3 will be coloured yellow; 4 balls

❷ 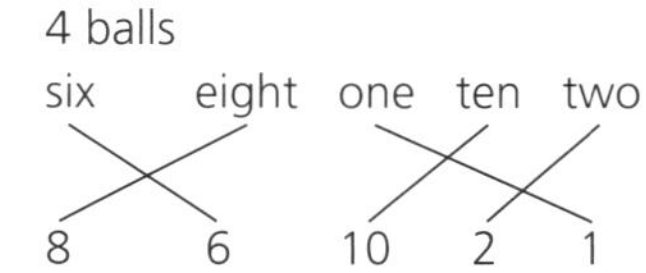

❸ 5

2:3

❶ The words will be traced and copied. The correct number of shapes will be drawn to match each number.

8 triangles, 11 circles, 12 ovals

3:1

10 (tomatoes)

❶ 7 ❷ 5 ❸  ❹ 12

5 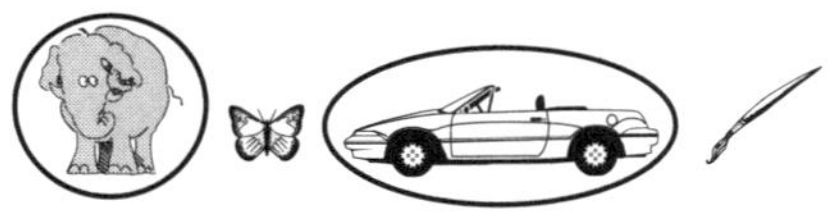

6 

7 Tuesday

8 11, 12, 13, 14, 15, 16, 17, 18, 19, 20

9 2, 4, 6, 8;   5, 6, 7, 8;

10 5 more lollipops will be drawn, making 15 altogether.

11 

12 12 leaves

3:2

10 (frogs)

1 0, 1, 2, 3, 4, 5, 6, 7, 8, 9, 10

2 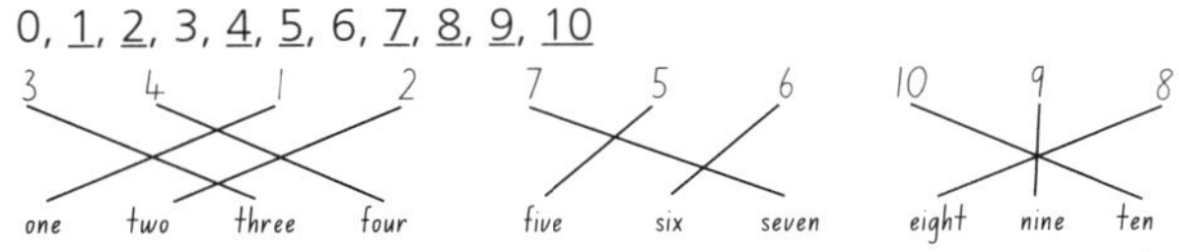

3 15, 16, 17, 18, 19, 20

4 20, 19, 18, 17, 16, 15

5 7

6 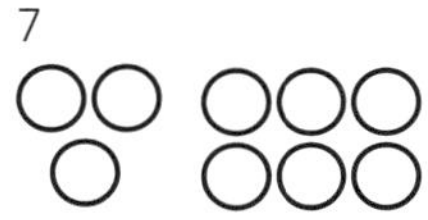 3 circles and 6 circles makes 9 circles.

3:3

1 Pictures will be drawn in the boxes. 3 and 4 makes 7

12 giraffes, 13 dragonflies, 10 penguins

4:1

4 (goats)

1 4 more balls will be drawn.

2 3 and 2 makes 5; 5

3 1st, 2nd, 3rd, 4th, 5th

4 5

5 Two squares will be drawn.

6 17, 16, 15, 14, 13

7 9 birds: 3 fly away, 6 birds left.

8 17, 19

9 7 o'clock

10 3 milkshakes will be coloured pink and 2 yellow. 5 are coloured altogether.

4:2

5 (fish)

1 1st, 2nd, 3rd, 4th, 5th

2 6 circles, 5 triangles, 2 rectangles

3 11, 13, 15, 17, 19

4:3

1 a 14 b 11 c 17 d 19 e 12 f 15

14 squares, 12 rectangles, 18 triangles

5:1

1 6 + 2 = 8

2 

3 3

4 1st, 2nd, 3rd, 4th, 5th

5 A triangle will be drawn.

6 16, 17, 18, 19, 20

7 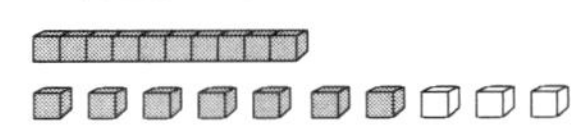

8 Answers will vary.

9 4 leaves will be coloured green and 2 will be coloured red; 6 leaves.

10 13, 20

5:2

Square, triangle, circle, rectangle.

1 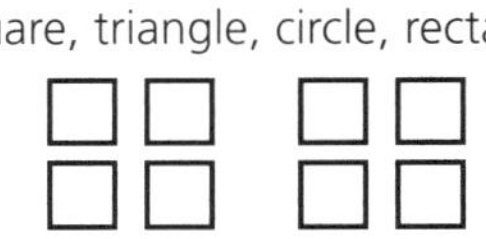 4 squares and 4 squares make 8 squares.

2

1	2	3	4	5	6	7	8	9	10
11	12	13	14	15	16	17	18	19	20

3 10, 11, 12, 13

5:3

10 (balloons)

1 a 12 b 13 c 15 d 20 e 19 f 17

9 frogs, 15 frogs, 8 frogs

6:1

1 5

2 2 rectangles will be drawn.

3 12, 11, 10, 9, 8, 7, 6, 5

4 19

5  Answers will vary.

6 2nd, 3rd, 4th, 5th

7 square

8 The missing numbers are in the shaded boxes.

12	13	14
7	8	9

 ISBN 978 1 4886 2177 2

❶ 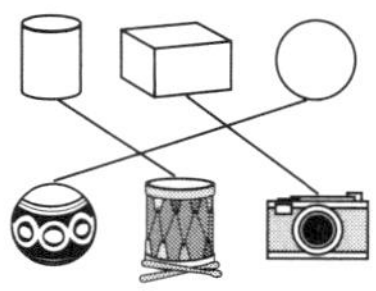

❷ 10 and 3 makes 13   10 + 3 = 13

6:2

❶ 10 and 4 = 14, 10 and 7 = 17

❷ 6, 9, 16, 19

❸ **a** 3, 4, 5, 6, 7, 8, 9, 10
b 13, 14, 15, 16, 17, 18, 19, 20
c 23, 24, 25, 26, 27, 28, 29, 30

6:3

11 (ants)

❶ **a** 4 **b** 6 **c** 12 **d** 2 **e** 6

37 squirrels

7:1

3 (balloons)

❶ 14, 15, 16, 17, 18

❷ 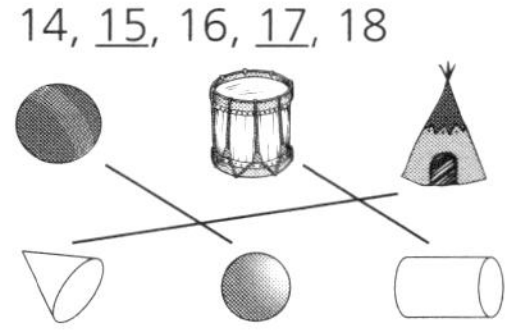

❸ 2 + 3 = 5

❹ 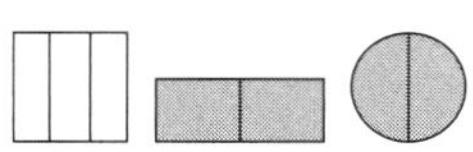

❺ 7

❻ 9 o'clock, 4 o'clock

❼ **a** 5 **b** 3 **c** 1 **d** platypuses **e** koalas

7:2

❶ 2, 4, 6, 8, 10; Add 2 is the rule.

❷ one, two, three, four, five, six

❸ Other answers may be possible.

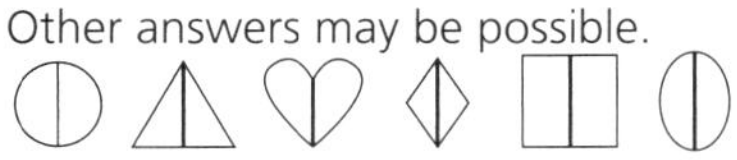

7:3

seven o'clock, five o'clock, nine o'clock, four o'clock, ten o'clock, six o'clock, eight o'clock, 12 o'clock, 11 o'clock

❶ 

48 roosters

8:1

❶ 6 + 4 = 10

❷ 3 o'clock

❸ 10 cent coin

❹ 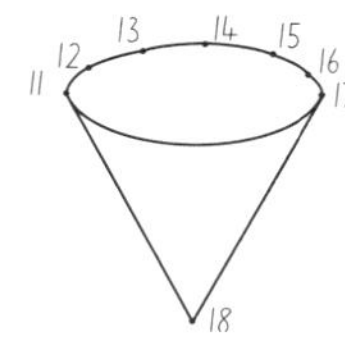

❺ Answers will vary.

❻ 5 trees altogether take away 2 is equal to 3.

❼ 10 + 6 = 16

❽ 20 cent coin

❾ **a** 10 **b** Scott **c** Christie **d** 3

8:2

6 (ants)

❶ The ice cream and the cone will be the same colour.
The milk carton and the prism will be the same colour.
The apple and the sphere will be the same colour.

❷ **a** 2 **b** 3 **c** 8 **d** 2

8:3

(double 2 =) 4

❶ **a** 10,10,10,10,10,10,10,10
b 8, 8, 8, 8, 8, 8, 8, 8

35 shells

9:1

3 + 2 = 5

❶ 50 cent coin

❷ Double 3 is 6, 3 + 3 = 6

❸ **a** 14, 15, 16, 17, 18   **b** 22, 21, 20, 19, 18

❹ 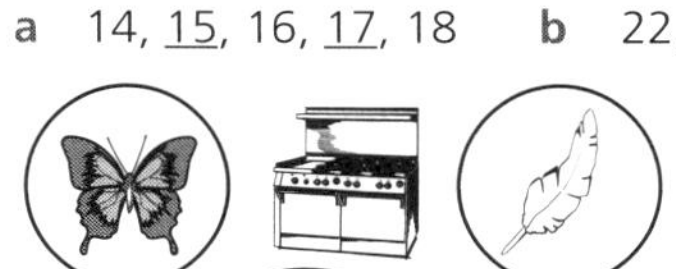

❺ 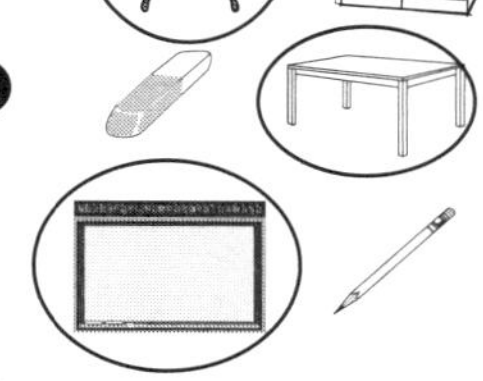

❻ 7 (paperclips)

❼ Monday

❽ 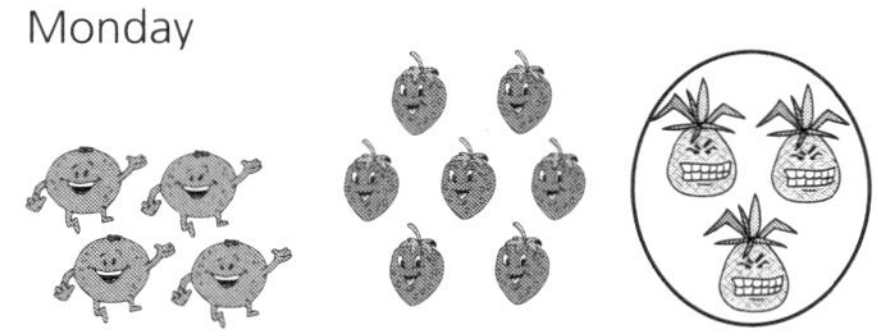

❾ 24, 26

❿ 26, 27, 28, 29, 30

⓫ 5 cent coin

⓬ 5, 10, 11, 14

9:2

14 (toy horses)

1 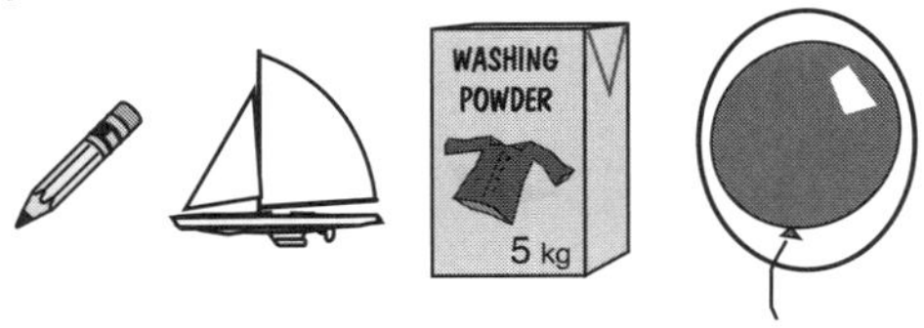

2 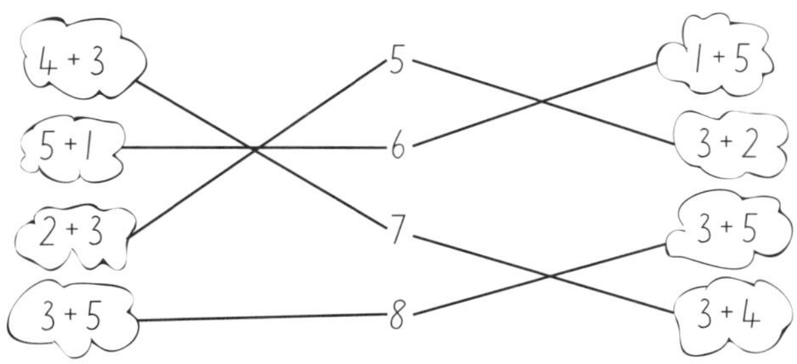

9:3

20 (circles)

1 a 8; 4 + 4 = 8 b 10; 5 + 5 =10
c 12; 6 + 6 = 12 d 16; 8 + 8 = 16
e 4; 2 + 2 = 4 f 14; 7 + 7 = 14

8 deer, 12 butterflies, 4 octopuses, 12 men, 16 girls

10:1

1 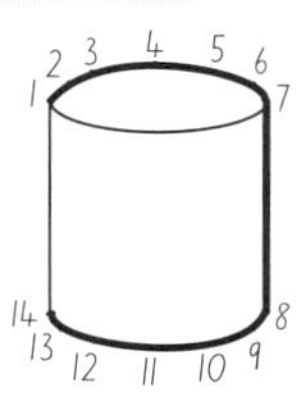

2 4 + 6 = 10 **3**  **4** 3 rubbers

5 A longer tail will be drawn. **6** one dollar coin

7 An oval will be drawn. **8** 3

9 The brick is heavier than the flowers.

10 two dollar coin

10:2

4 + 5 = 9

1 9, 4, 13, 5, 5 **2** 5, 10, 9, 7, 8, 10, 5, 10

3 

10:3

(double 3 =) 6

1 a 1 square b 8 rectangles c 4 triangles d 0 circles
e 4 ovals

2 The shapes will be coloured so that similar shapes are the same colour.

32 elephants

11:1

9 (ducks)

1 10 + 6 = 16 **2** 20, 30, 40, 50, 60

3 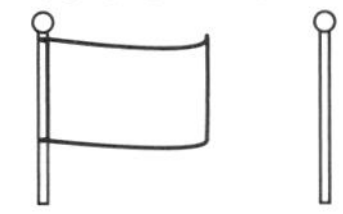

4 Answers will vary. **5** The 1st pencil will be coloured.

6 two dollar coin **7** 9

8 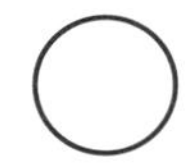 **9** The brick is heavier than the book.

10 4 tens; 40

11 The $1 and $2 coins will be coloured yellow.

11:2

10, 20, 30, 40, 50, 60, 70, 80

1 Lia has 7 flowers. Bob has 3 flowers. Lia has 4 more flowers than Bob. 7 – 3 = 4

2 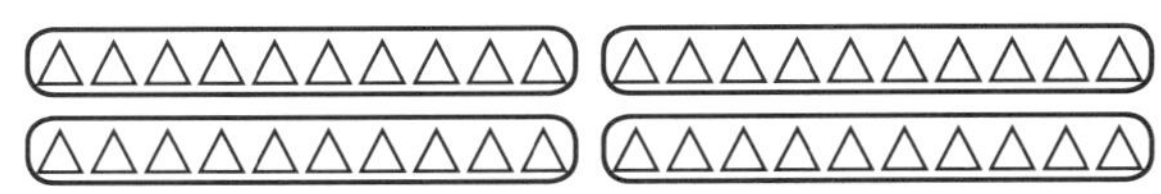

40 triangles

3

5c	10c	20c	50c
five cents	ten cents	twenty cents	fifty cents

11:3

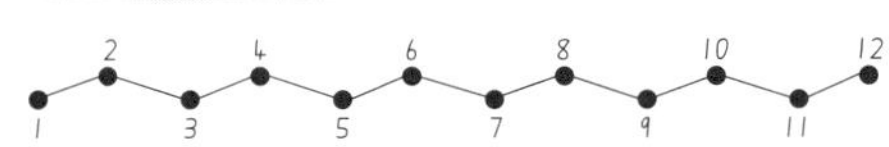

1 20, 41 **2** 12, 36

3

1	2	3	4	5	6	7	8	9	10
11	12	13	14	15	16	17	18	19	20
21	22	23	24	25	26	27	28	29	30
31	32	33	34	35	36	37	38	39	40
41	42	43	44	45	46	47	48	49	50

6 bears, 10 moose, 5 roosters

12:1

18 (squares)

1 4 + 3 = 7

2 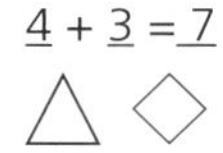

3 80, 70, 60, 50, 40

4 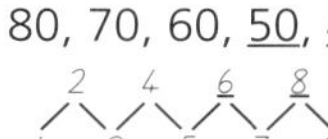 **5** 3

6 a 4 b 7 c 11 d 18 e 8 **7** 3 more squares; 3

8 The woman is to the right of the cashier, behind the trolley.

9 7, 8

10 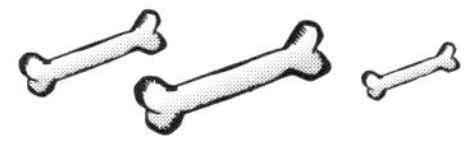

2 3 1

12:2

20 (buttons)

1 

2 The $2 coin will be coloured red. The 5 cent coin will be coloured blue.

3 

4 5, 6, 4, 7

12:3

square, circle, rectangle, triangle

1 2 squares, 3 circles, 1 rectangle and 1 triangle will be drawn on the grid.

8 swordfish, 19 swans, 12 turkeys

13:1

8 – 5 = 3

1 6

2 **a** 10, 20, 30, 40, 50, 60
b 90, 80, 70, 60, 50, 40, 30, 20

3 7 tens, 70

4 **a** 15 **b** 10 **c** 12 **d** 3 **e** 19

5 11, 10, 9, 8, 7

6 The girl is on the left of the pony.

7 **a** 80 **b** 20 **c** 60

8 2 more squares; 2

9 5 squares and 5 hexagons

10 Thursday

13:2

ball, can, yoyo, pen

1 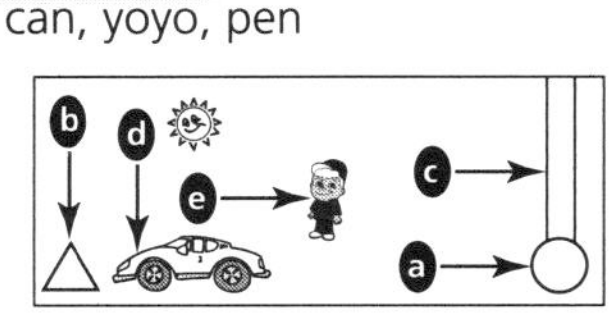

2 **a** 20, 19, 18, 17, 16, 15, 14, 13, 12, 11, 10
b 6, 7, 8, 9, 10, 11, 12, 13, 14, 15, 16

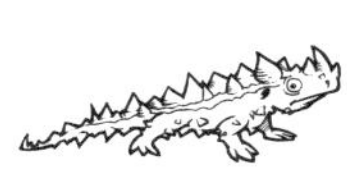

13:3

dog

1 27, 50

2 31, 20

3

1	2	3	4	5	6	7	8	9	10
11	12	13	14	15	16	17	18	19	20
21	22	23	24	25	26	27	28	29	30
31	32	33	34	35	36	37	38	39	40
41	42	43	44	45	46	47	48	49	50

8 dinosaurs, 10 snakes, 12 frogs

14:1

8 – 3 = 5

1 9,12,12, 7

2 11 o'clock 11:00

3 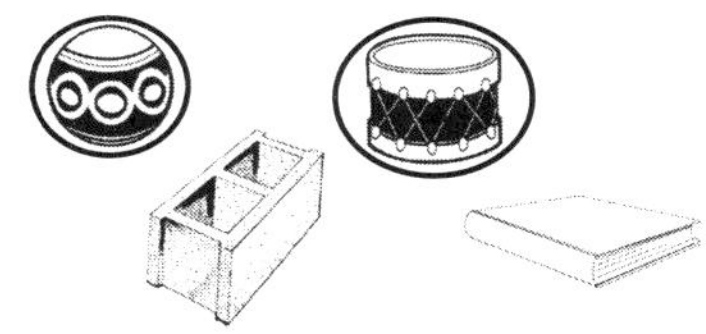

4 6 squares and 1 hexagon

5 10, 20, 30, 40, 50, 60

6 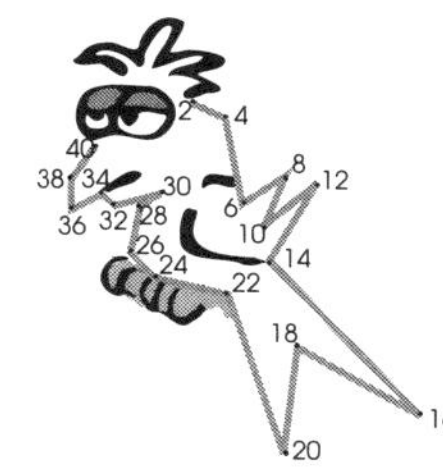

7 

8 **a** two **b** four **c** six **d** nine **e** ten

9 5

14:2

1 10 tens 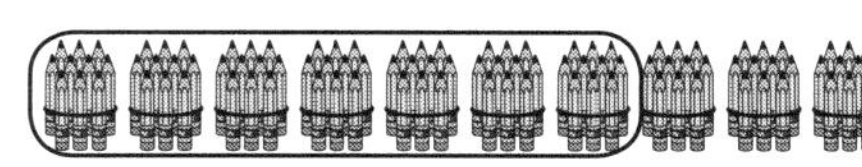

2 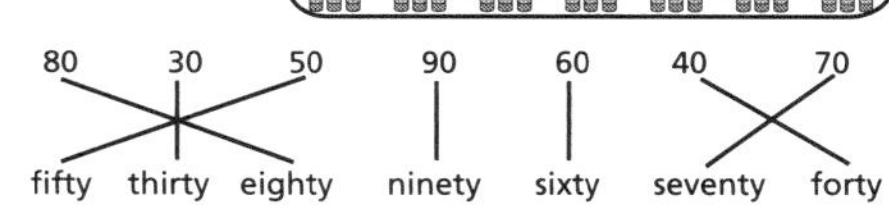

3 Answers will vary.

4 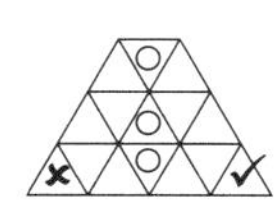

14:3

5 + 4 = 9

1 **a** 7 **b** 15 **c** 16 **d** 10

12 seals, 15 sheep, 18 sharks

15:1

□ 4 sides, 4 corners, △ 3 sides, 3 corners, ○ 0 corners, 0 sides, ▭ 4 corners, 4 sides, ⬡ 6 corners, 6 sides, ◊ 4 corners, 4 sides

1 7, 11, 7, 10

2 6 o'clock, 11 o'clock

3 6 tens 5 ones = 65

4 **a** 7, 6, 5, 4
b 12, 11, 10, 9
c 18, 17, 16, 15

❺ 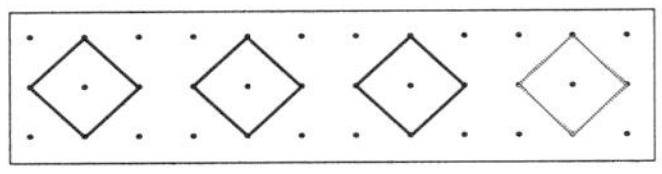

A square has been used.

❻ triangle ❼ 14 ❽ 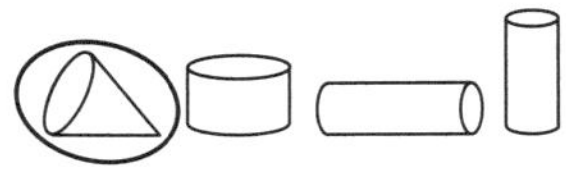

❾ 5 + 5 = 10; Double 5 = 10

❿ Guess = (Answers will vary.)
Number = 16

15:2

22, 43, 25, 78

❶ 

❷ Tom has 8 cars. Madeline has 5 cars. Tom has 3 more cars.

❸ 7 tens 5 ones = 75
4 tens 3 ones = 43
6 tens 1 one = 61

15:3

6 (men)

❶ 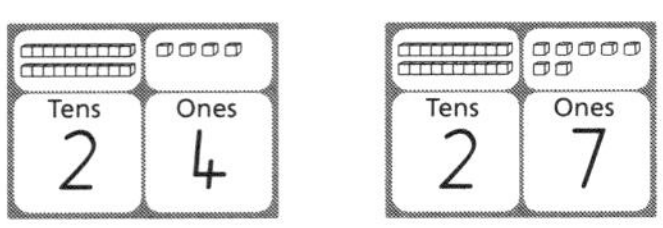

6 flamingoes, 9 horses, 12 owls

16:1

bath tub

❶ a 9, 8, 7, 6 b 14, 13, 12, 11 c 20, 19, 18, 17

❷ Answers will vary. ❸ 5 and 5 make 10.

❹ a 3 birds b 5 trees c 2 more trees d 2

❺ 13, 11 ❻ A rectangle and a triangle will be drawn.

❼ The third bucket will be ticked. ❽ 13 – 5 = 8

❾  ❿ 6, 6

16:2

99

❶ a 1 ten 1 one = 11 b 2 tens 3 ones = 23
c 5 tens 9 ones = 59 d 2 tens 2 ones = 22
e 5 ones 1 one = 51 f 5 tens 5 ones = 55
g 3 tens 4 ones = 34

❷ 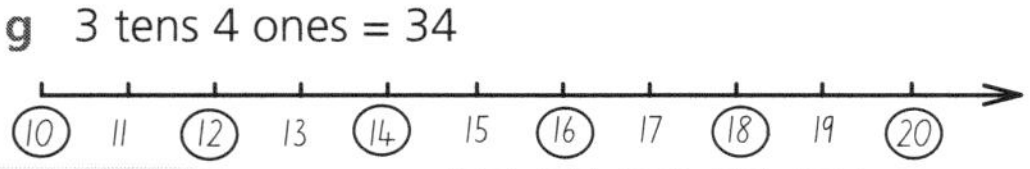

16:3

22, 32, 45

❶ a 22 b 51 c 30 d 44

7 spiders, 9 cats, 8 elephants

17:1

❶ 7 days ❷ 3, 6, 7, 9 ❸ 8, 10, 12, 14, 16

❹ 8

❺ 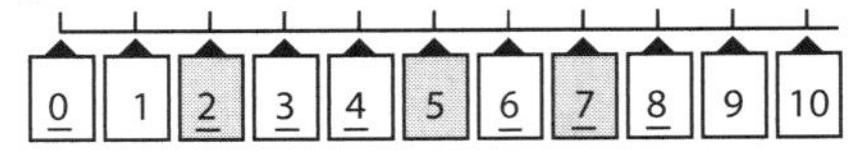

❻ Estimate = (Answers will vary.) Number = 17

❼ Answers will vary. ❽ 5 + 5 = 10

❾ A square will be drawn. ❿ Answers will vary.

⓫ a 12 b 15 c 18 d 17

17:2

3 + 7 = 10

❶ 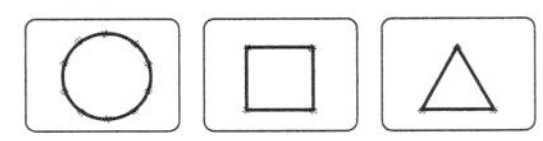

❷ 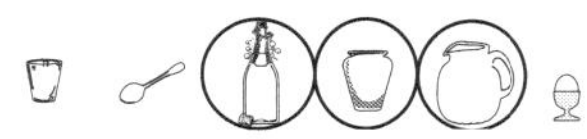

The glass holds more than the spoon.
The spoon holds less than the eggcup.

❸  ❹ A pear

17:3

20 (brushes)

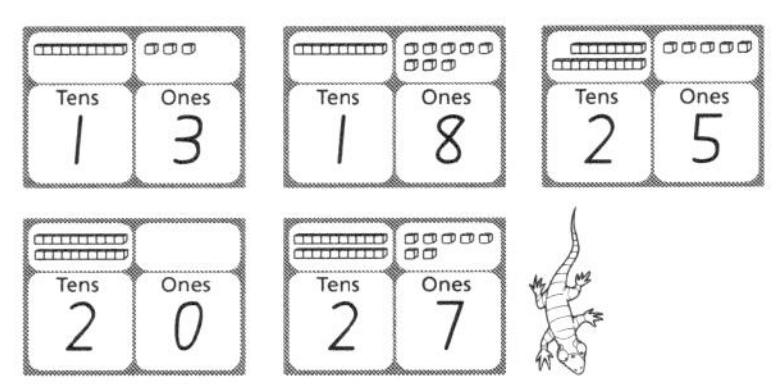

16 horses, 9 scorpions, 18 birds

18:1

❶ 10 and 6 = 16 ❷ 69, 80 ❸ 4 + 6 = 10

❹ 

❺ 3, 7 ❻ Answers will vary. ❼ 11, 15, 18, 20

❽ a twenty-nine b eighteen ❾ 7 + 4 = 11

❿ This is a zigzag line. ⓫ 10 – 7 = 3

⓬ 8, 8 ⓭ Answers will vary.

18:2

3 (lizards)

❶ 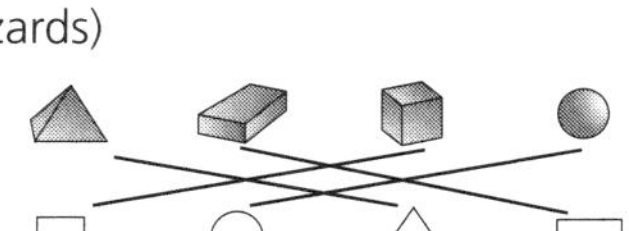

❷ Sunday, Monday, <u>Tuesday</u>, Wednesday, <u>Thursday</u>, Friday, <u>Saturday</u>

❸ Answers will vary.

18:3

46, 52

❶ a 

b 

c 

13 dogs, 14 ducks, 12 platypuses

19:1

3 + 5 = 8

❶

11	12	13	14	15
16	17	18	19	20

❷ Answers will vary. Answers could include: <u>0</u> + <u>9</u> = 9, <u>1</u> + <u>8</u> = 9 and <u>2</u> + <u>7</u> = 9

❸ 3 : 00

❹ This is a wavy line.

❺ 92, 91, <u>90</u>, <u>89</u>, <u>88</u>

❻ (10) 11 (12) (15) 16 (17) (19) 20 (21) (27) 28 (29)

❼ forty-two, fifty-six

❽ a half past 11 b half past 5

❾

21	22	23	24	25
26	27	28	29	30

❿ a  b 

⓫ a 10 b 20 c 12 d 13

19:2

❶ 

❷ 

12:00 4:00 9:00 2:00

❸ a 32 b 74 c 98 d 15 e 50 f 21

19:3

9 (shapes)

❶ Answers will vary. A shape will be drawn that uses 4 dots (rectangle), 6 dots (hexagon) and 8 dots (octagon).

8 rhinoceroses, 32 rabbits, 14 roosters

20:1

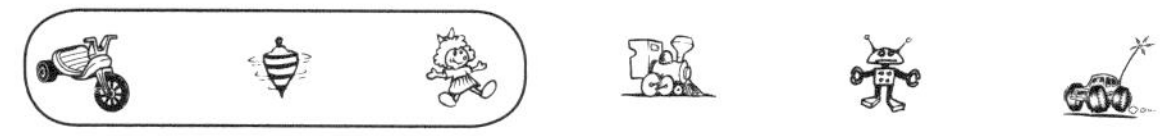

❶ Answers will vary. Answers could include: <u>0</u> + <u>7</u> = 7, <u>1</u> + <u>6</u> = 7 and <u>2</u> + <u>5</u> = 7

❷ Answers will vary. 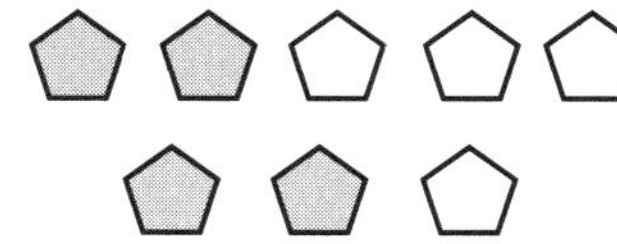

❸ a 19, <u>18</u>, <u>17</u>, <u>16</u> b 14, <u>13</u>, <u>12</u>, <u>11</u> c 12, <u>11</u>, <u>10</u>, <u>9</u>

❹ a half past 8 b half past 9

❺ 40, 50, 60, <u>70</u>, <u>80</u>

❻ 63, 62, <u>61</u>, <u>60</u>, <u>59</u>

❼ a b 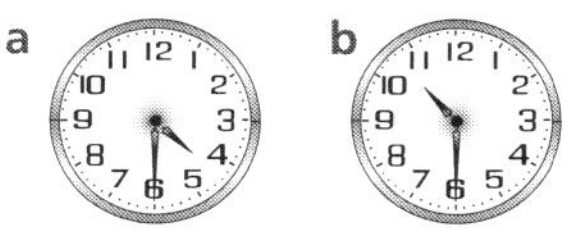

❽ 10, 10, 11, 11

❾ 9

❿ 5 more circles: 5 + <u>5</u> = 10 10 – <u>5</u> = 5

⓫ 27, 28, 29, <u>30</u>, <u>31</u>, <u>32</u>

20:2

full, half full, empty, quarter full, three-quarters full

❶ 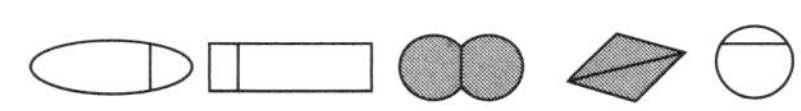

❷ Answers will vary.

❸ a 10, 20, 30, <u>40</u>, <u>50</u>, 60, <u>70</u>, <u>80</u>, <u>90</u>, 100

b 74, 75, 76, <u>77</u>, <u>78</u>, <u>79</u>, <u>80</u>, 81, <u>82</u>, <u>83</u>

c 47, 48, 49, <u>50</u>, <u>51</u>, <u>52</u>, <u>53</u>, <u>54</u>, 55, <u>56</u>

20:3

5 (suns)

❶ a 4 b 7 c 6 d 5

8 kangaroos, 11 monkeys, 14 beavers

21:1

2, 4, 6, <u>8</u>, <u>10</u>, <u>12</u>, <u>14</u>, <u>16</u>, <u>18</u>

❶ 16

❷ 3 more circles: 6 + <u>3</u> = 9 9 – 6 = <u>3</u>

❸ Half of the group will be circled.

❹ a 18, <u>17</u>, <u>16</u>, <u>15</u>, <u>14</u>

b 15, <u>14</u>, <u>13</u>, <u>12</u>, <u>11</u>

c 20, <u>19</u>, <u>18</u>, <u>17</u>, <u>16</u>

❺ seventeen, twenty-one

6 a 7, 9, 11, 13, 15, 17
b 12, 10, 8, 6, 4, 2
c 40, 50, 60, 70, 80

7 a Rule: Add 2
b Rule: Take away 2
c Rule: Add 10

8 a half past 6 b half past 11

9 63, 78

10 4 : 30

21:2

4 + 6 = 10

1 Sunday Saturday

2 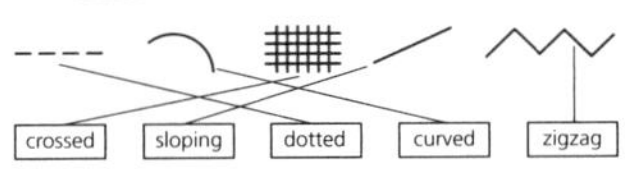

3 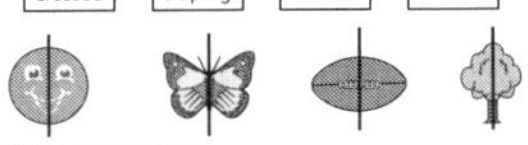

21:3

Answers will vary. 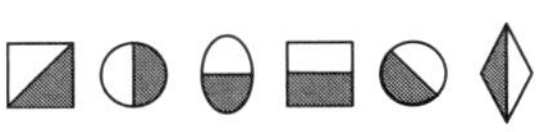

1 13 − 5, 7 + 2, 12 − 4, 4 + 8, 16 − 8, 2 + 6, 14 − 6, 5 + 3, 16 − 9

12 squirrels, 36 snails, 14 spiders

22:1

2 (horses)

1 6 + 4 = 10 10 − 6 = 4

2 a half past 4 b half past 12

3 5 + 6 = 11 6 + 5 = 11
7 + 8 = 15 8 + 7 = 15

4 

5 5, 10, 15, 20, 25

6 Answers will vary.

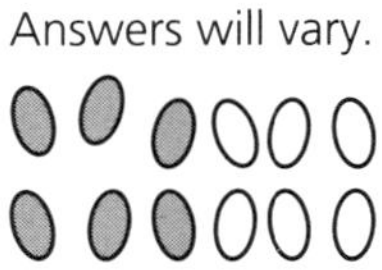

7 25, 19

8 4 + 4 + 4 = 12 3 rows of 4 = 12

9 15

10 Estimates will vary. 50 is a good estimate.
Groups of ten = 5

11 19 − 8 = 11

12 Answers will vary. 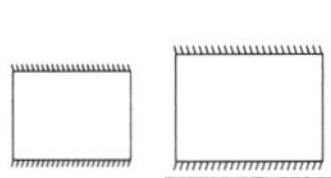

22:2

4 + 3 = 7

1 

21 animals

2 Tuesday 3, Thursday 5, Wednesday 4, Saturday 7, Monday 2, Friday 6, Sunday 1

3 a 5, 10, 15, 20, 25, 30, 35, 40, 45
b 10, 20, 30, 40, 50, 60, 70, 80, 90

22:3

9 (shells)

1 a 2 rows of 7 = 14 7 + 7 = 14
b 3 rows of 6 = 18 6 + 6 + 6 = 18
c 2 rows of 5 = 10 5 + 5 = 10
d 3 rows of 5 = 15 5 + 5 + 5 = 15

10 seahorses, 22 bears, 13 goats

23:1

rectangular prism, cylinder, cube

1 2 rows of 6 = 12 6 + 6 = 12

2 10

3 2nd, 3rd, 4th, lst

4 ◁ ○

5 10 and 8 equals 18.

6 8 + 9 = 17
9 + 8 = 17

7 20, 22, 24, 26, 28

8 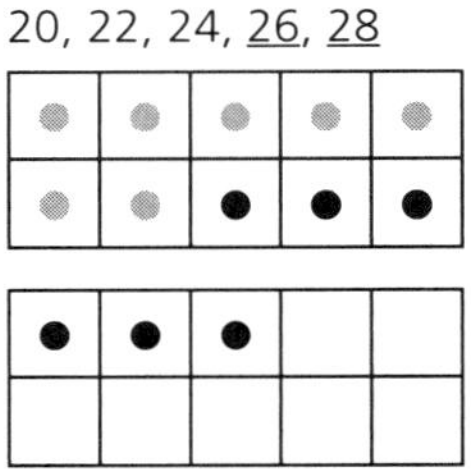
7 + 6 = 7 + 3 + 3
= 10 + 3
= 13

9 7 (days)

10 

11 eighty-three — 83
ninety-two — 92
thirty-eight — 38
twenty-nine — 29

23:2

10, 20, 30, 40, 50, 60, 70, 80, 90

1 a 5 (birds) b 8 (cats) c 10 (dogs)
d 6 (fish) e 3 (rabbits) f 1 (horse)
g dogs h horses

23:3

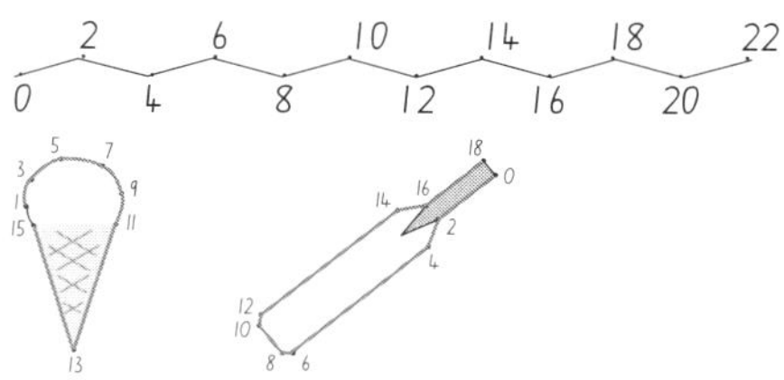

8 pterodactyls, 20 brontosaurus, 14 tyrannosaurus rex

24:1

❶ The pencil is 7 paperclips long. ❷ 79

❸ 21, 34 ❹ March

❺

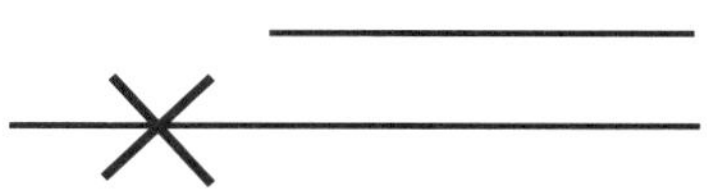

❻ triangles and a square

❼ 5 + 6 = 11   6 + 5 = 11

❽

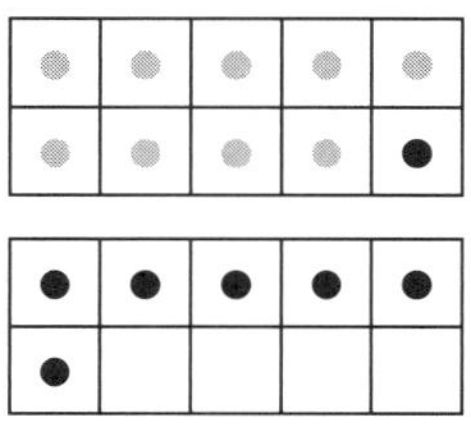

9 + 7 = 9 + 1 + 6
= 10 + 6
= 16

❾ 89 ❿ A rhombus will be drawn.

⓫

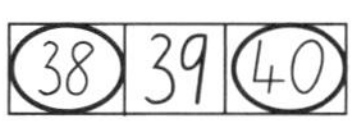

24:2

6 + 4 = 10

❶ 10 and 3 = 13   10 and 8 = 18
10 and 5 = 15   20 and 1 = 21
20 and 4 = 24   20 and 6 = 26
30 and 9 = 39   30 and 2 = 32

❷ 20, 31, 44, 63, 82

24:3

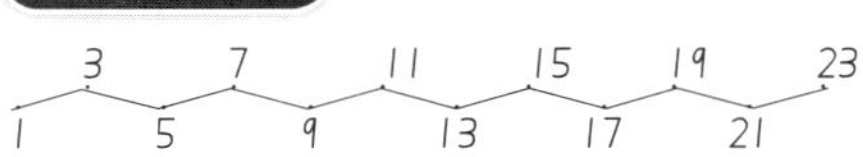

❶ a 2, 4, 6, 8, 10   b 1, 3, 5, 7, 9
c 10, 8, 6, 4, 2   d 5, 7, 9, 11, 13
e 6, 8, 10, 12, 14   f 9, 7, 5, 3, 1

9 dolphins, 15 eagles, 16 dogs

25:1

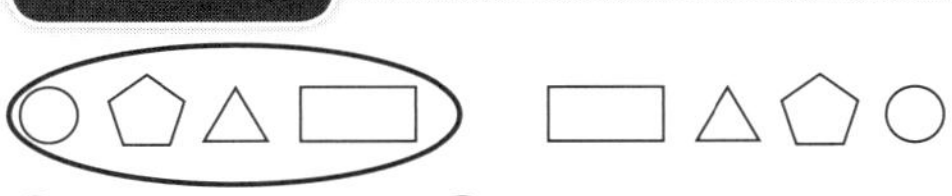

❶ 7 ❷ 51

❸ a 12, 14, 16, 18, 20
b 5, 10, 15, 20, 25

❹ The 50c and 20c coins will be ticked. ❺ May

❻ 33, 34 ❼ 59 will be circled.

❽ 6 tens 3 ones

❾ A rectangle will be drawn: 4 sides, 4 corners

❿ a 79   b 40   c 83

⓫ There are 2 more ovals than triangles.

⓬ Answers will vary. One answer could be 91.

25:2

7 tens = 70

❶ 1 ten 2 ones = 12   2 tens 3 ones = 23
7 tens 5 ones = 75   3 tens 2 ones = 32

❷ 1 January   2 February   3 March
4 April   5 May   6 June
7 July   8 August   9 September
10 October   11 November   12 December

25:3

30, 40, 50, 60, 70, 80, 90, 100

❶

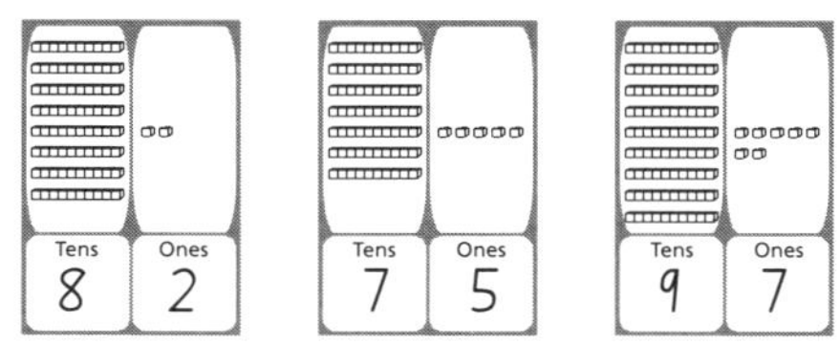

16 camels, 18 hens, 18 cows

26:1

9 – 3 = 6

❶ 47 ❷ 16, 94 ❸ 94

❹ a 5, 7, 9, 11, 13, 15
b 0, 3, 6, 9, 12, 15
c 63, 62, 61, 60, 59

❺

❻ 10 ❼ a 60   b 21   c 100

❽ a 15   b spiders   c horses ❾ 50 = 5 tens 0 ones

❿ a 14, 15, 16, 17 so 14 + 3 = 17
b 17, 18, 19, 20 so 17 + 3 = 20

⓫ 4:30

⓬

41	42	43	44	45
46	47	48	49	50

⓭ 39

26:2

1. January, April, December
2. Sunday; 1 week = 7 days
3. September; 1 year = 12 months
4. 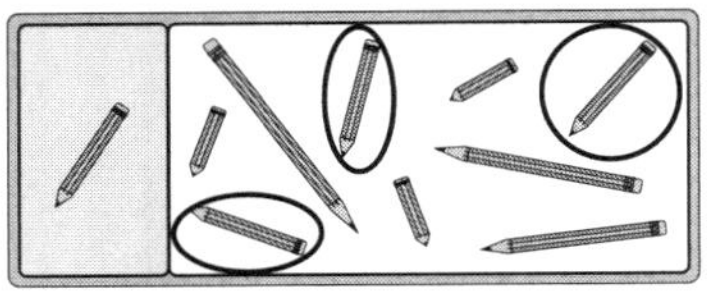

26:3

1, 2, 3, 4, 5, 6

1. a 0 + 5 = 5 b 1 + 4 = 5
   c 4 + 1 = 5 d 2 + 3 = 5
   e 5 + 0 = 5

18 turtles, 22 sharks, 12 dolphins

27:1

6 + 3 = 9

1. 79, 80
2. 17
3. a 12, 13, 14 so 12 + 2 = 14
   b 15, 16, 17 so 15 + 2 = 17
4. 10 : 30
5. 4
6. a 12, 10, 8, 6, 4
   b 20, 30, 40, 50, 60
   c 5, 7, 9, 11, 13, 15
7. 44 = 4 tens 4 ones
8. 
9. a 16, 15, 14, 13 so 16 − 3 = 13
   b 12, 11, 10, 9 so 12 − 3 = 9
10. A triangle has 3 sides. An octagon has 8 sides.
11. 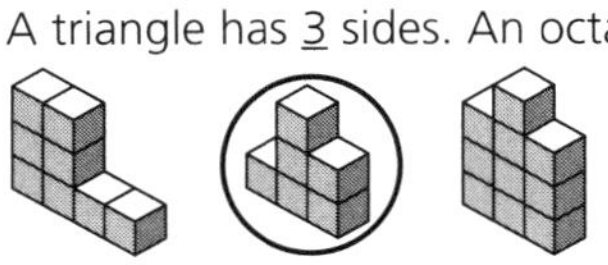
12. no, yes, no

27:2

1. a 5 b 3 c 6 d 4 e 3 f 1

27:3

7, 6, 7, 5, 10, 8, 12

1. a 5 + 4 = 9 b 0 + 6 = 6
2. a 5 + 2 = 7 b 4 + 5 = 9
   c 6 + 3 = 9 d 1 + 9 = 10

12 birds, 42 butterflies, 14 bison

28:1

3

1. 97
2. 73, 91
3. 
4. 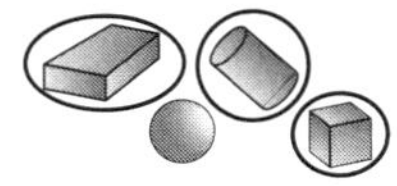
5. 12 + 4 = 16 16 − 4 = 12
6. 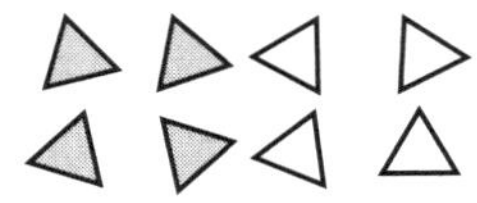
7. Answers will vary.
8. a 15, 14, 13 so 15 − 2 = 13
   b 19, 18, 17 so 19 − 2 = 17
9. hexagon. It has 6 sides. It has 6 corners.
10. 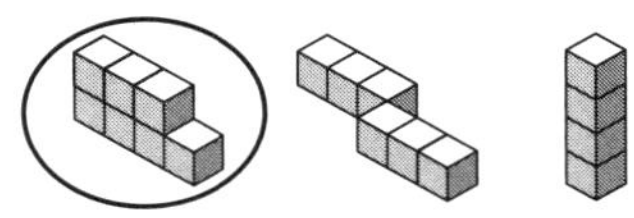
11. 5 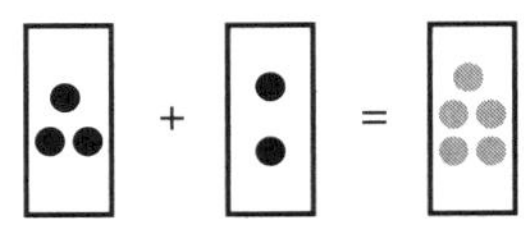
12. Ist, 3rd

28:2

9 − 4 = 5

1. January, February, March, April, May, June, July, August, September, October, November, December
2. Answers will vary.
3. star, rhombus (or diamond), circle
4. 5, 15, 9, 19, 9, 19, 9, 19

28:3

16 (circles)

1. a (6) b 9 c 4 d 7 e 1 f 5

Half of each group will be coloured. Answers will vary.

29:1

1. 7:30
2. 10
3. 7 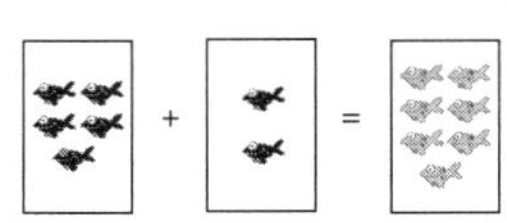
4. 
5. 3 + 6 = 9 9 − 3 = 6 9 − 6 = 3

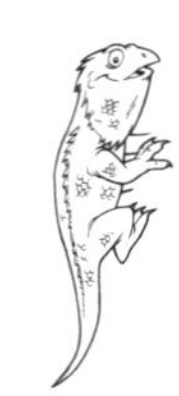

 ISBN 978 1 4886 2177 2

❻ 22 = 2 tens 2 ones

❼ 

❽ 9 + 5 = 14   14 – 5 = 9

❾ 4, 7, 2, 5

❿ a 63 will be circled.
b 90 will be circled.

⓫ Answers will vary.

29:2

❶ a 12 b May c 3rd d December e March

❷ 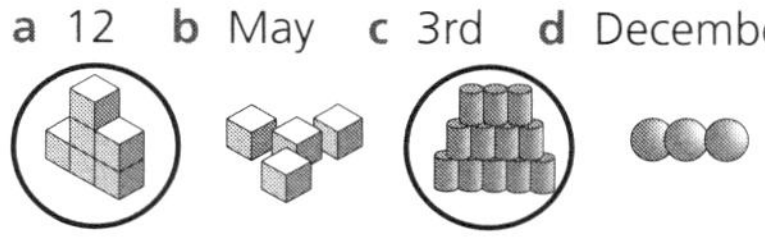

6 4 12 3

❸ The 6 stacked cubes will be coloured red.

29:3

10 – 3 = 7

❶ a 5 b 3 c 6 d 4 e 4 f 2

❷ A pattern will be made by colouring circles.

30:1

6 – 3 = 3

❶ 6 + 4 = 10   10 – 4 = 6

❷ unlikely

❸ rectangle

❹ Answers will vary.

❺ yes

❻ 46, 47

❼ 90

❽ 4 + 8 = 12   12 – 4 = 8   12 – 8 = 4

❾ 39

❿ 

⓫ The Corny Flakes box will be crossed.

⓬ 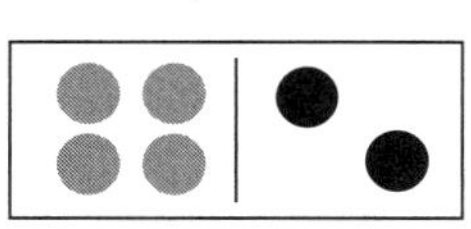

= 6

4 + 2 = 6

⓭ clockwise

30:2

❶ 

full   half full   nearly full

❷ one dollar   fifty cents   twenty cents   two dollars

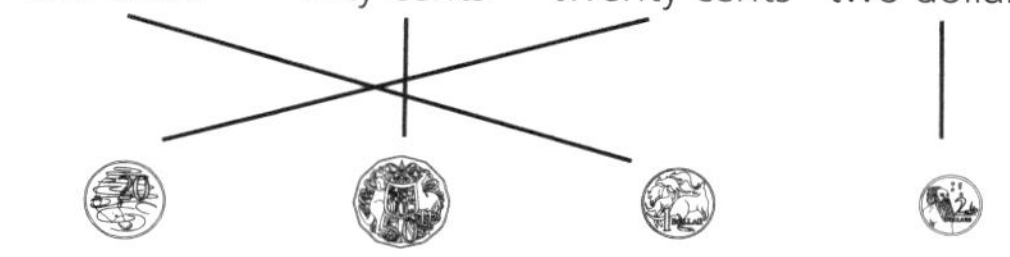

❸ 

$5.00 $10.00 $20.00 $50.00 $100.00

30:3

23, 24, 25, 26; 57, 58, 59, 60

❶ a 28, 30, 32, 34, 36
b 63, 61, 59, 57, 55
c 37, 35, 33, 31, 29
d 75, 77, 79, 81, 83
e 44, 46, 48, 50, 52
f 81, 79, 77, 75, 73

70 spiders

31:1

2

❶ 10 + 6 = 16   16 – 6 = 10

❷ Answers will vary.

❸ 12

❹ 1st, 2nd, 3rd, 4th

❺ 

❻ 

❼ 93

❽ 61 will be circled.

❽ 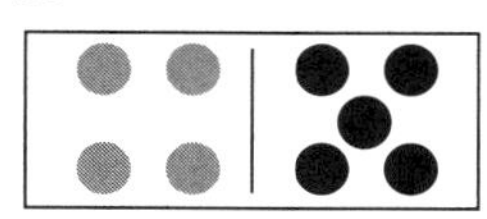

= 9

4 + 5 = 9

❾ anticlockwise

❿ a 15   b 18

⓫ 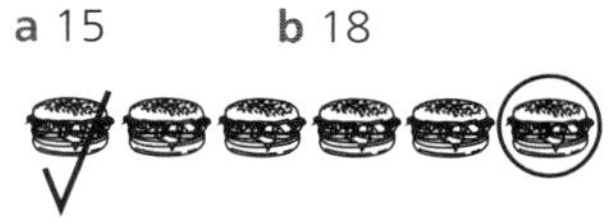

⓬ Answers will vary.

31:2

❶ a park b beach c home d pool e beach

❷ 5, 9, 10, 9, 8, 9, 10, 8, 10

❸ 1st, 2nd, 3rd, 4th, 5th

31:3

7 + 8 = 15

❶ a 6, 8, 10
b 8, 10, 12
c 1, 3, 5
d 12, 14, 16
e 17, 19, 21
f 10, 12, 14

70 snails

32:1

1, 2, 3, 4, 5

❶ 

❷ **a** 12 **b** 16

❸ The teddy bear will be circled.

❹ ❺ 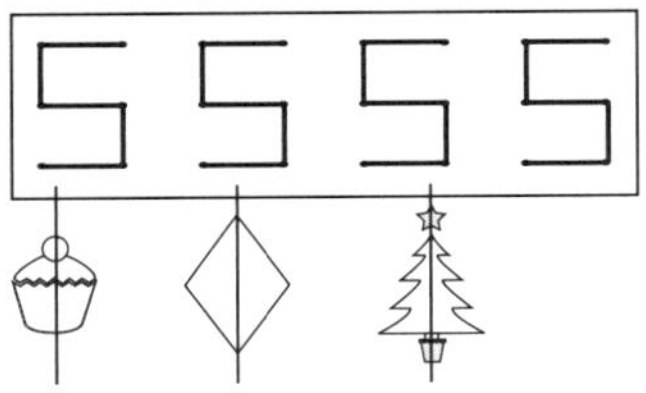

❻ 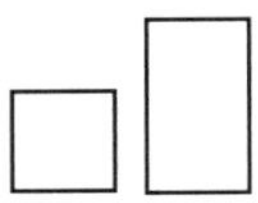 ❼ 88

❽ 6 + 4 = <u>10</u> 4 + 6 = <u>10</u> 3 + 7 = <u>10</u>
7 + 3 = <u>10</u> 6 + 1 + 3 = <u>10</u>

❾ 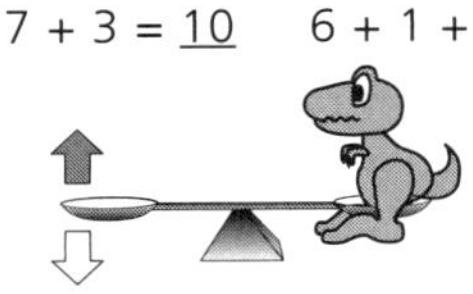

❿ 8 + <u>7</u> = 15 15 − 8 = <u>7</u>

⓫ 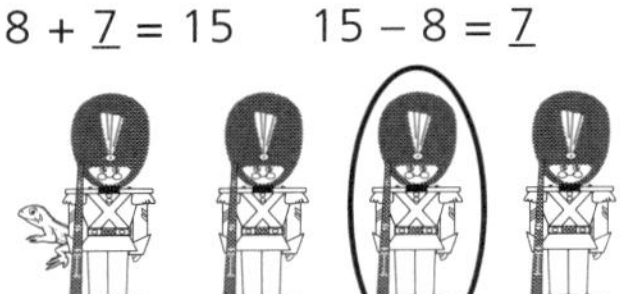

⓬ 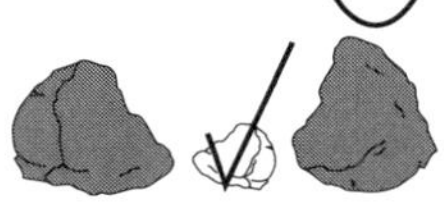

32:2

❶ **a** 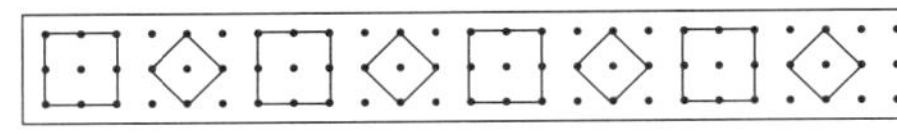

b 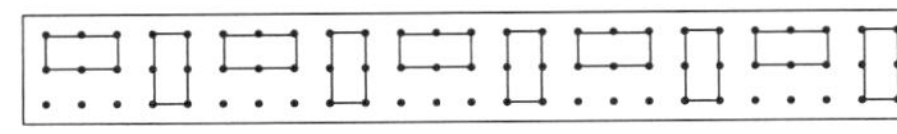

❷ 8 − 4 = <u>4</u> 9 − 6 = <u>3</u> 10 − 5 = <u>5</u>
3 − 3 = <u>0</u> 5 − 0 = <u>5</u> 10 − 4 = <u>6</u>
9 − 2 = <u>7</u> 7 − 1 = <u>6</u> 10 − 7 = <u>3</u>

❸ **a** 39 = <u>3</u> tens <u>9</u> ones **b** 62 = <u>6</u> tens <u>2</u> ones

32:3

square, circle, diamond, rectangle

❶ The top shapes will be coloured and copied below.

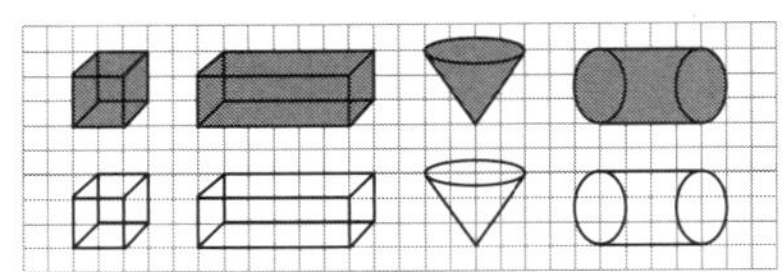

Half of each group will be coloured.

Multiple-choice Questions

❶ twenty-seven ❷ 54 ❸ 39 ❹ 8 ❺ 14

❻  ❼ triangle ❽ hexagon ❾ cube

❿ drink bottle

 ISBN 978 1 4886 2177 2

17:2

☐ + ☐ = ☐

❶ Join the dots to draw a circle, a square and a triangle.

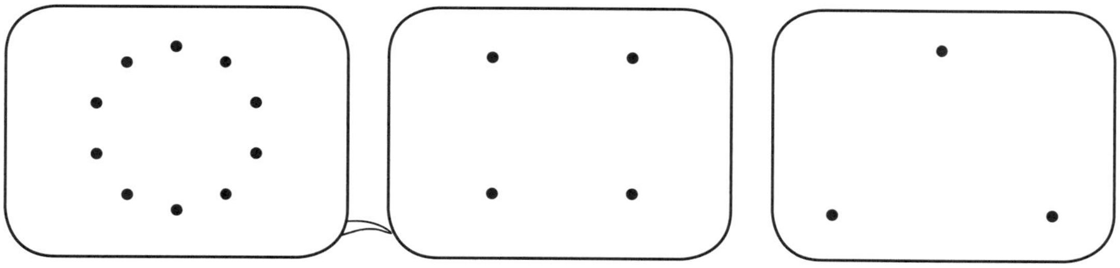

❷ Circle the containers that hold more than the glass.

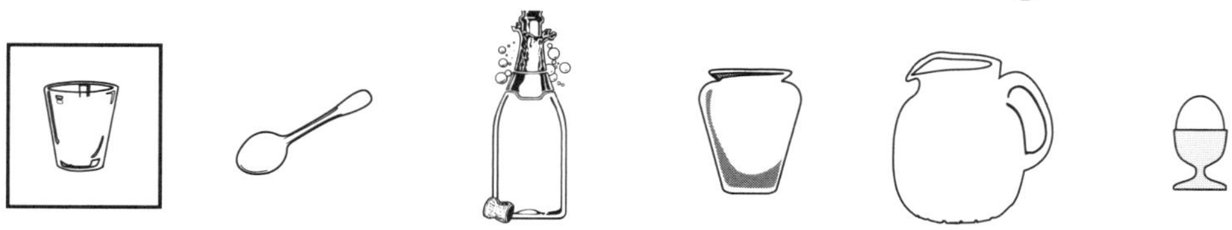

The glass holds **more / less** than the spoon.

The spoon holds **more / less** than the eggcup.

❸ Finish this pattern.

❹ What is the 4th piece of fruit in question 3? ______________________

17:3

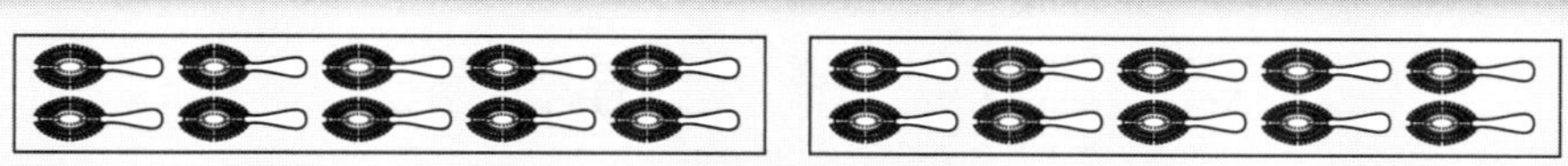

❶ Complete these number cards.

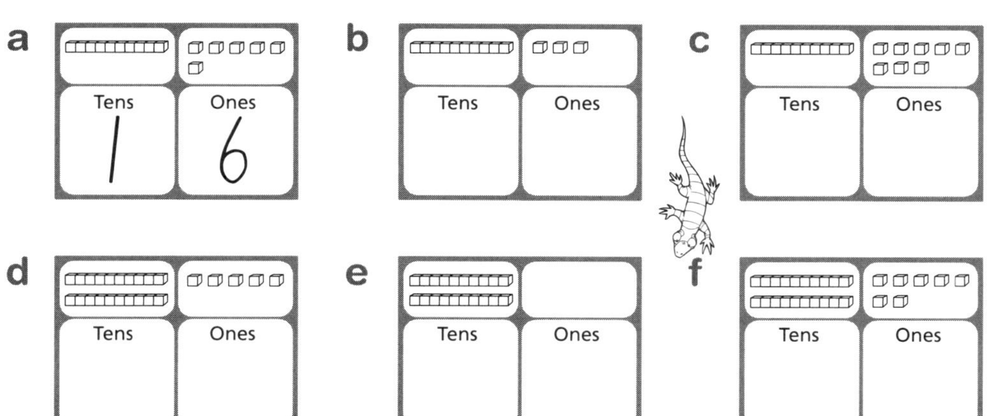

 • *AUSTRALIAN SIGNPOST MATHS 1 MENTALS* • ISBN 978 1 4886 2177 2

18:1

❶

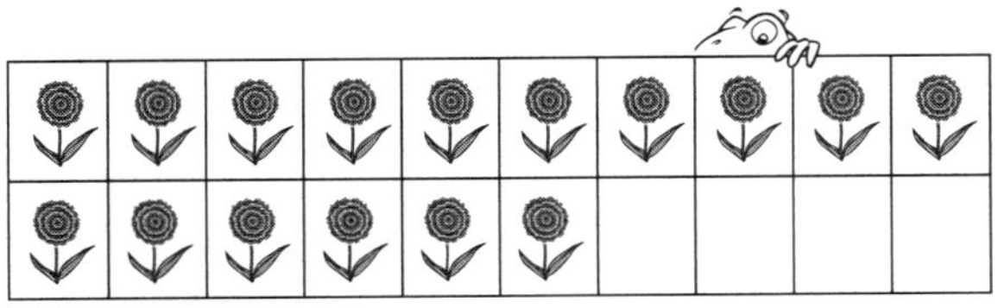

_______ and _______ = _______

❷ The number before:

70 _______ 81 _______

❸

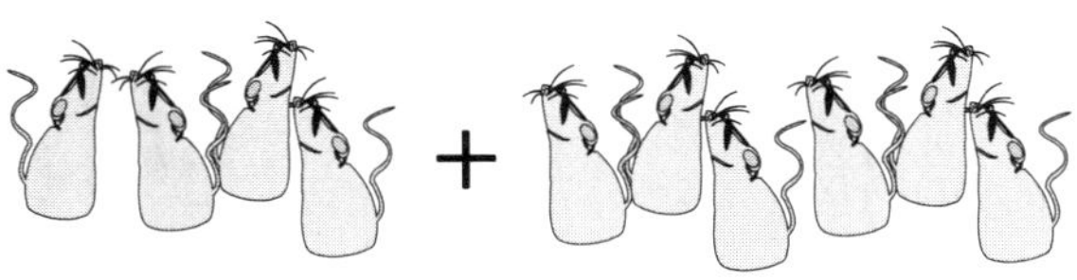

____ + ____ = _____

❹ Circle the animal with the greatest mass.

❺ 

10 subtract 7 = _______

10 subtract 3 = _______

❻ Complete: I might _______________

_____________________________.

❼ Write these numbers in order.

18, 15, 11, 20

_____, _____, _____, _____

❽ Write the name for:

a 29 _______________________

b 18 _______________________

❾

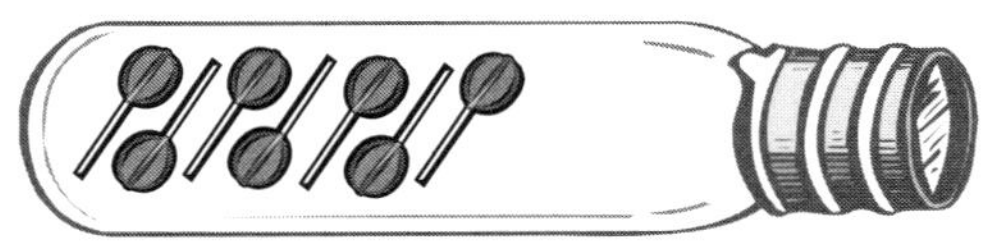

There are 7 lollies in a jar.
4 more are put into the jar.
How many lollies altogether?

____ + ____ = _____

❿

This is a z_______________ line.

⓫

Complete:

____ − ____ = ____

⓬ 3 + 5 = ____ 5 + 3 = ____

⓭ What day is it?

____

 ISBN 978 1 4886 2177 2

18:2

❶ Match each 3D object with the shape of its face.

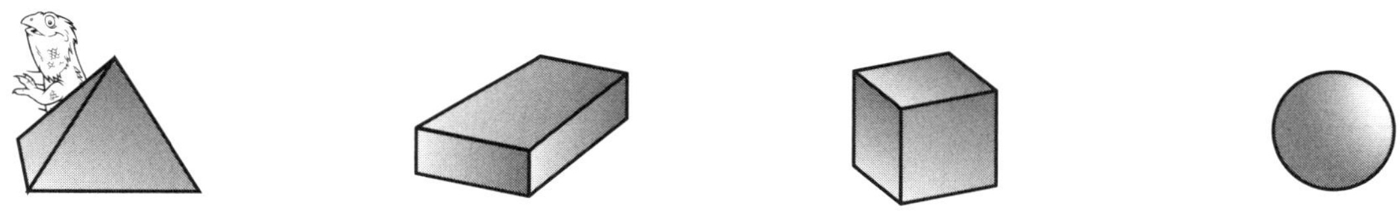

❷ Sunday, Monday, ____________, Wednesday,

____________, Friday, ____________.

❸ On the scales, draw a picture of something that will be:

lighter balanced heavier

183

❶ Complete these number cards.

a

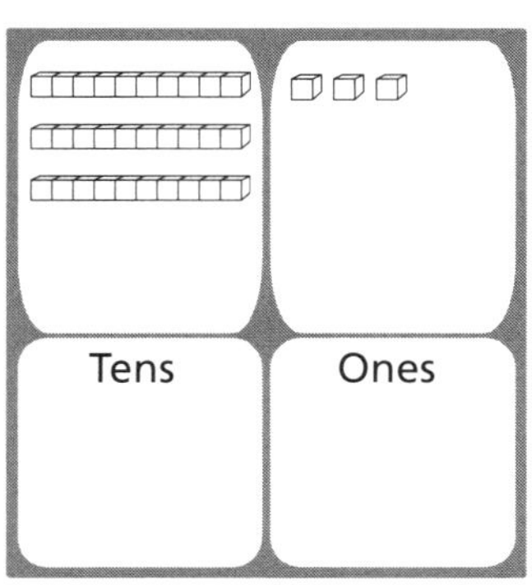

b

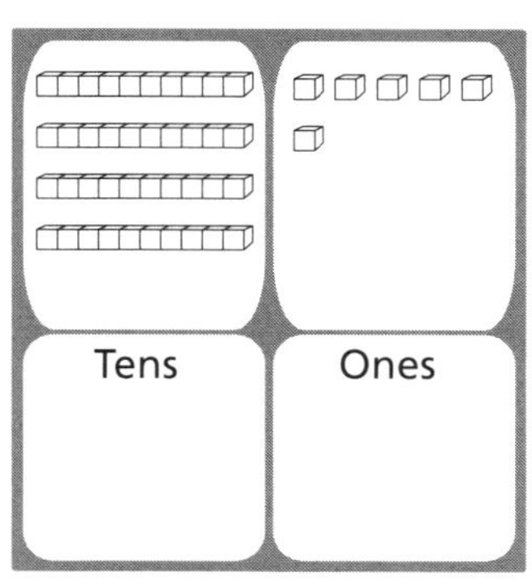

c

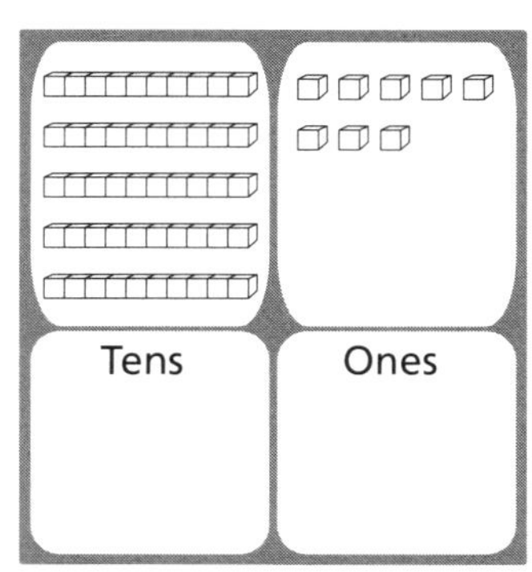

19:1

 ☐ + ☐ = ☐

❶ Complete this grid.

	12	13		
				20

❷ Write three different sums.

_____ + _____ = 9

_____ + _____ = 9

_____ + _____ = 9

❸ Write the digital time.

❹ 

This is a w________________ line.

❺ 92, 91, _____, _____, _____

❻ What comes **before** and **after**?

	11	

	16	

	20	

	28	

❼ Write the word for:

42 ____________________

56 ____________________

❽ Write the time shown:

a 

half past ☐

b 

half past ☐

❾ Fill in the missing numbers.

Colour the numbers that have a 2 in them.

	22	23		
26				30

❿ Show these times.

a 

half past 8

b 

half past 2

⓫ Write the numeral for each:

a ten _____ **b** twenty _____

c twelve _____ **d** thirteen _____

 ISBN 978 1 4886 2177 2

19:2

❶ Circle to match the cube to an object.

❷ Fill in the analogue times on these clock faces.

12 : 00	4 : 00	9 : 00	2 : 00

❸ Write the numeral for each.

a thirty-two ________ **b** seventy-four ________

c ninety-eight ________ **d** fifteen ________

e fifty ________ **f** twenty-one ________

19:3

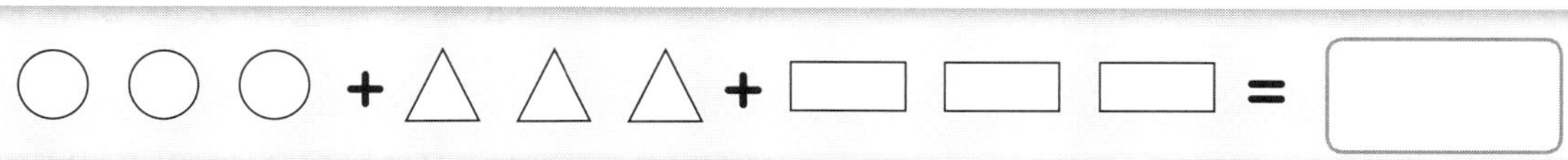

❶ Draw a shape on this grid that uses:

4 dots 6 dots 8 dots

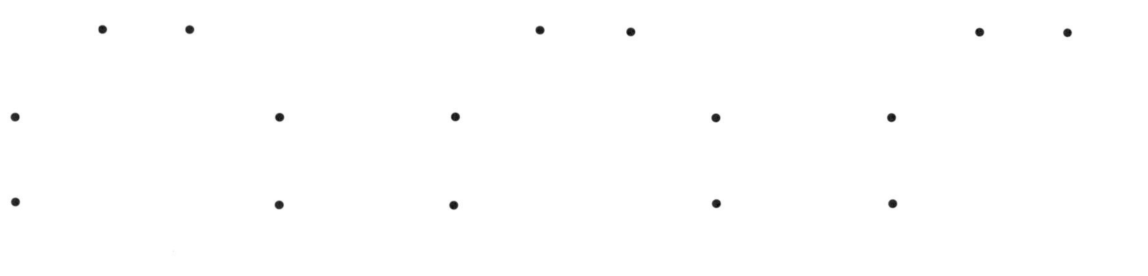

❶ Write 3 different sums.

_____ + _____ = 7

_____ + _____ = 7

_____ + _____ = 7

❷ Colour half of these pentagons.

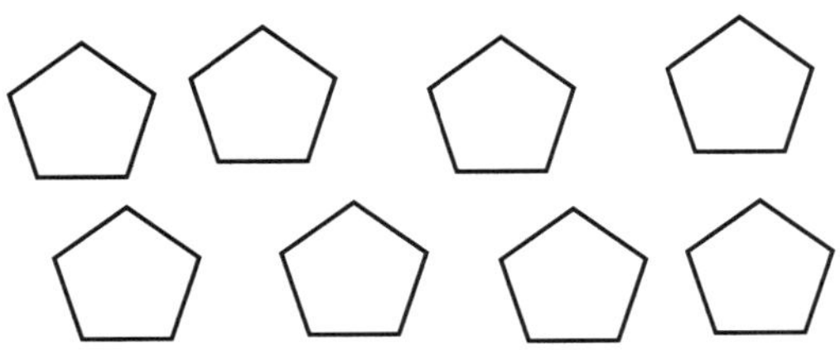

❸ Count back from:

a 19, _____, _____, _____

b 14, _____, _____, _____

c 12, _____, _____, _____

❹ Write the time shown:

a  b 

half past ☐ half past ☐

❺ 40, 50, 60, _____, _____

❻ 63, 62, _____, _____, _____

❼ Show these times.

a  b 

half past 4 half past 10

❽ 6 + 4 = _____ 4 + 6 = _____

6 + 5 = _____ 5 + 6 = _____

❾ 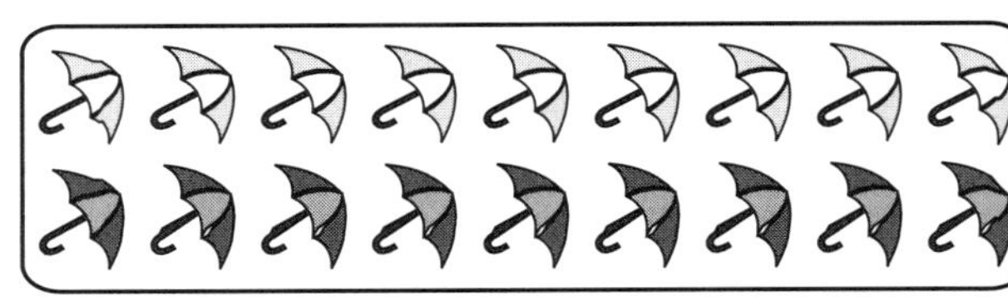

18 take away 9 equals _____.

❿ How many more to make 10 circles?

5 + _____ = 10

10 − _____ = _____

⓫ Complete the number pattern.

27, 28, 29, _____, _____, _____

20:2

❶ Colour the shapes that have been cut into halves.

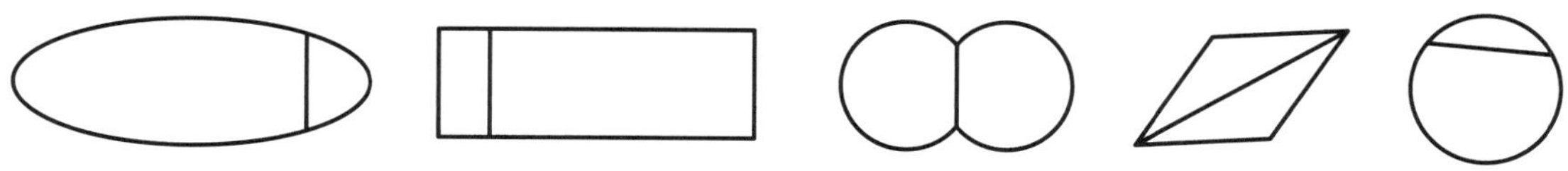

❷ On the balance scales draw lighter things.

A ____________ has a smaller mass than a book.

A ____________ has a smaller mass than a bottle.

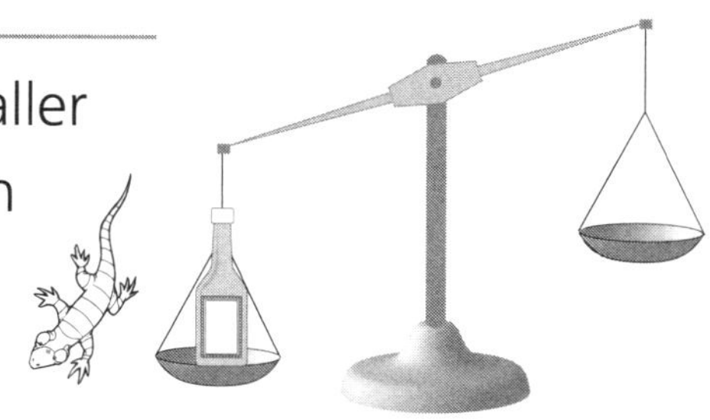

❸ Write the missing numbers.

a 10, 20, 30, ____, ____, 60, ____, ____, ____, 100

b 74, 75 76, ____, ____, ____, ____, 81, ____, ____

c 47, 48, 49, ____, ____, ____, ____, ____, 55, ____

20:3

❶ There are 10 coins in each group.
How many are covered by the hand?

a

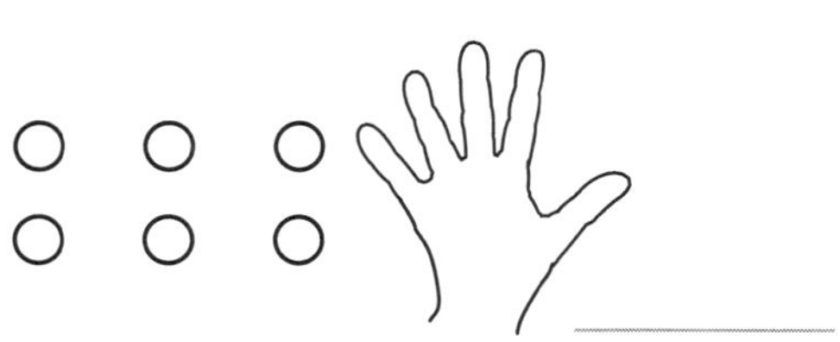

____

b

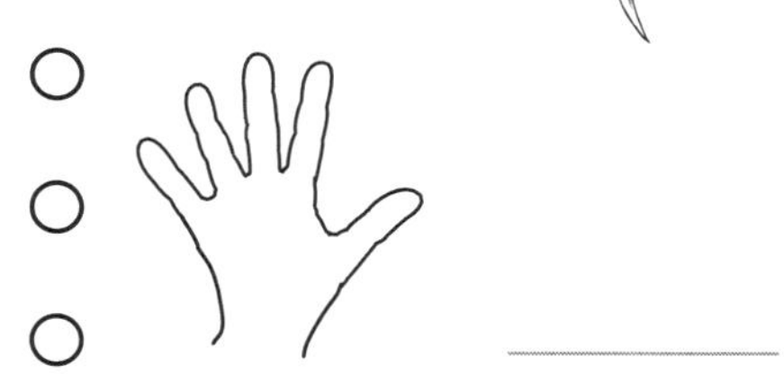

____

c

____

d

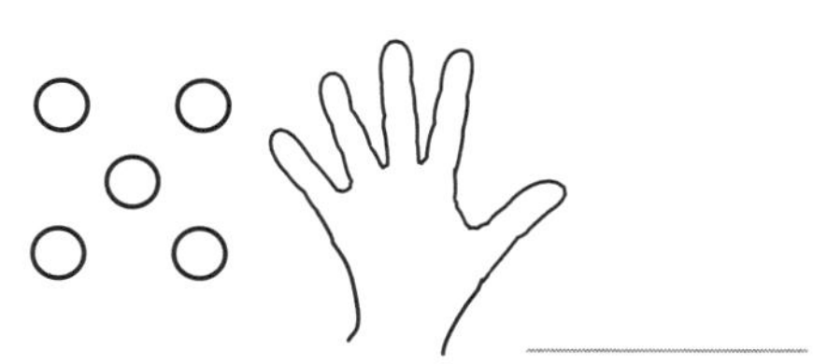

____

21:1

2, 4, 6, ____, ____, ____, ____, ____, ____

❶ We were given 20 lollies.

We ate 4.

How many are left? ____

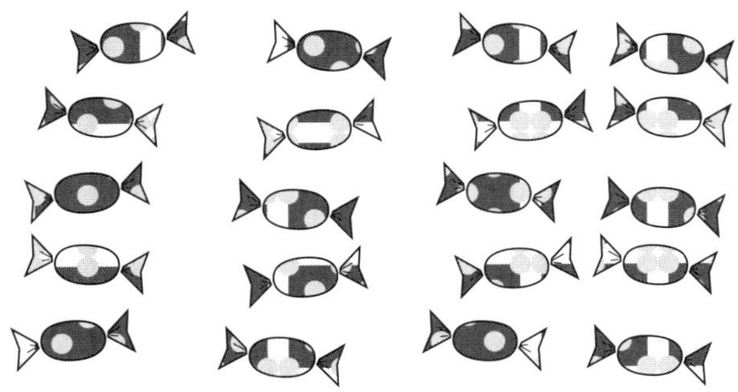

❷ How many more to make 9 circles?

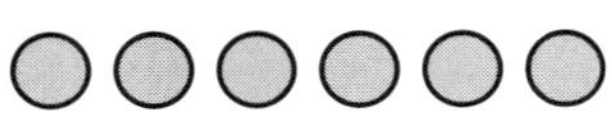

6 + ____ = 9

9 – 6 = ____

❸ Circle one half of this group.

❹ Count back from:

a 18, ____, ____, ____, ____

b 15, ____, ____, ____, ____

c 20, ____, ____, ____, ____

❺ Write the names:

17 ______________________

21 ______________________

❻ Finish the patterns.

a 7, 9, 11, 13, ____, ____

b 12, 10, 8, 6, ____, ____

c 40, 50, 60, ____, ____

❼ Write the rule for each part in Question 6.

a Rule: ______________________

b Rule: ______________________

c Rule: ______________________

❽ Complete each label.

a

b

half past ☐ half past ☐

❾ Write the numeral for:

sixty-three ____

seventy-eight ____

❿ Write the digital time for half past 4.

☐ : ☐

 ISBN 978 1 4886 2177 2

21:2

4 + 6 = ☐

❶ Circle the weekend days.

Sunday Monday Tuesday Wednesday Thursday Friday Saturday

❷ Match the names with the lines.

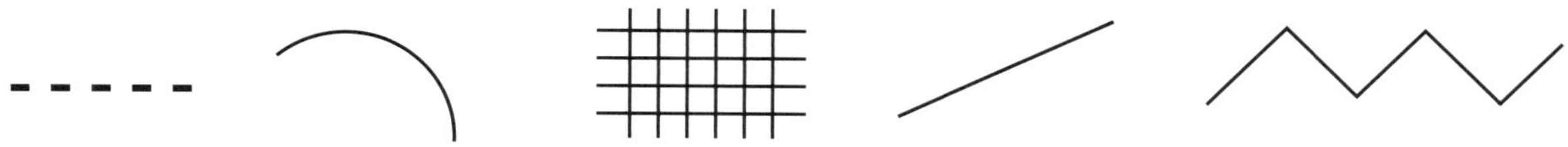

crossed	sloping	dotted	curved	zigzag

❸ Draw a line to cut each picture in half.

21:3

Shade half of each shape.

❶ Colour the boxes that give the answer 8.

13 − 5	7 + 2	12 − 4
4 + 8	16 − 8	2 + 6
14 − 6	5 + 3	16 − 9

1

6 + ____ = 10

10 − 6 = ____

2 Complete each label.

a

b

half past ☐   half past ☐

3 5 + 6 = ____   6 + 5 = ____

7 + 8 = ____   8 + 7 = ____

4 Circle the fifth doll from the left.

5 5, 10, 15, ____, ____

6 Colour half of these ovals.

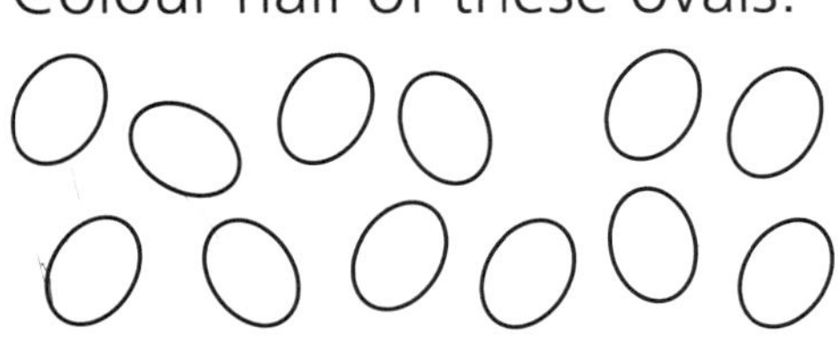

7 Write the numeral for:

twenty-five ____

nineteen ____

8 3 rows of 4

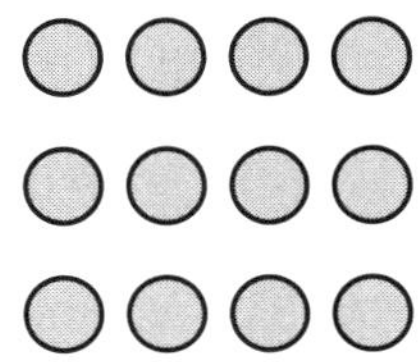

4 + ____ + ____ = ____

____ rows of ____ = ____

9 19 minus 4. ____

10 Estimate how many, then circle groups of ten.

Estimate = ____

Groups of ten = ____

11 19 lollies, 8 eaten.
How many left?

____ − ____ = ____

12 Draw a mat wider than this one.

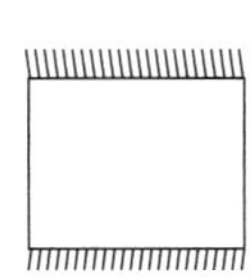

 • *AUSTRALIAN SIGNPOST MATHS 1 MENTALS* • ISBN 978 1 4886 2177 2

22:2

 ☐ + ☐ = ☐

❶ **Animals at the Zoo**

Circle the smallest group of animals.

Underline the largest group of animals.

How many animals altogether? ______

❷ Show the days of the week in order, from 1 to 7.

Tuesday	Thursday	Wednesday	Saturday	Monday	Friday	Sunday
☐	☐	☐	☐	☐	☐	1

❸ **a** 5, 10, 15, ____, ____, ____, ____, ____, ____

b 10, 20, 30, ____, ____, ____, ____, ____, ____

22:3

 = ☐

❶ **a** 

____ rows of ____ = ______

____ + ____ = ____

b 

____ rows of ____ = ______

____ + ____ + ____ = ______

c 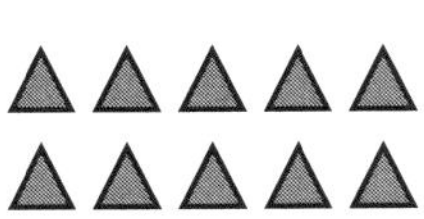

____ rows of ____ = ______

____ + ____ = ____

d 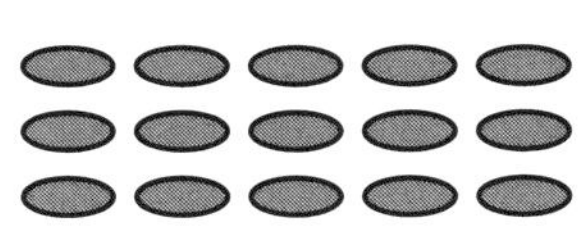

____ rows of ____ = ______

____ + ____ + ____ = ______

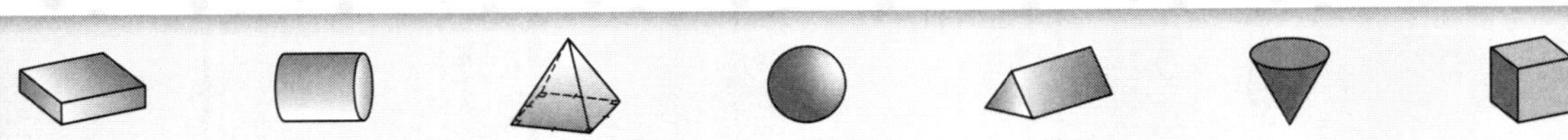

❶ 2 rows of 6 = ______

______ + ______ = ______

❷ How many place-value ones blocks would be the same length as the tens block?

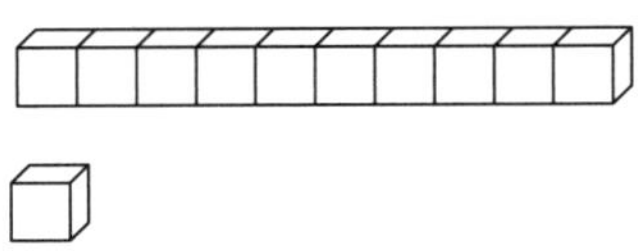

______

❸ Order from shortest to tallest.

______ ______ ______ *1st*

❹ Continue this pattern.

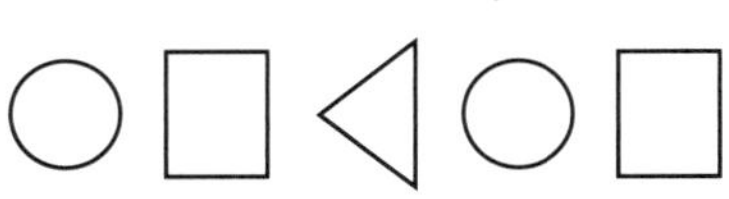 ______ ______

❺ 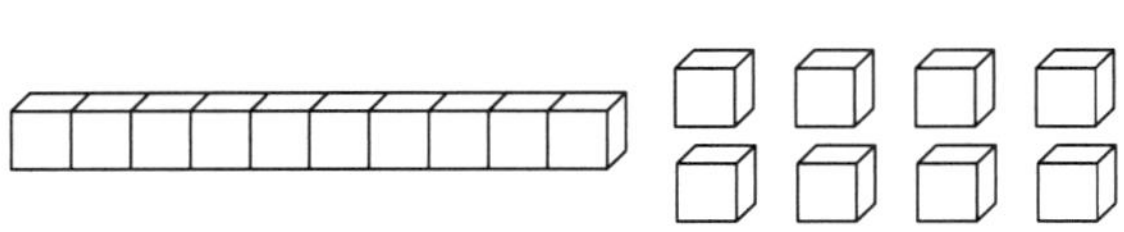

______ and ______ equals ______.

❻ 8 + 9 = ______ 9 + 8 = ______

❼ *20, 22, 24,* ______, ______

❽ Draw dots, then complete each number sentence.

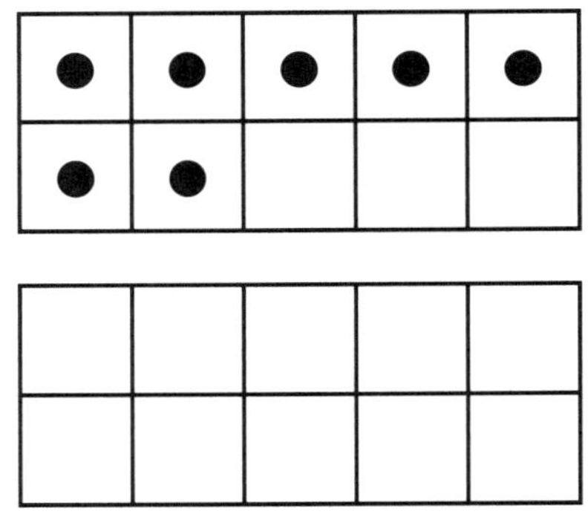

7 + 6 = 7 + ______ + ______

= ______ + ______

= ______

❾ How many days in one week?

______

❿ Circle the one that takes less time.

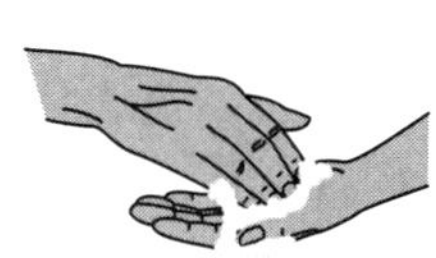

Wash Hands

Do the Dishes

⓫ Match the names and numerals.

eighty-three 38
ninety-two 29
thirty-eight 83
twenty-nine 92

23:2

10, 20, 30, ______, ______, ______, ______, ______, ______

❶

Animals

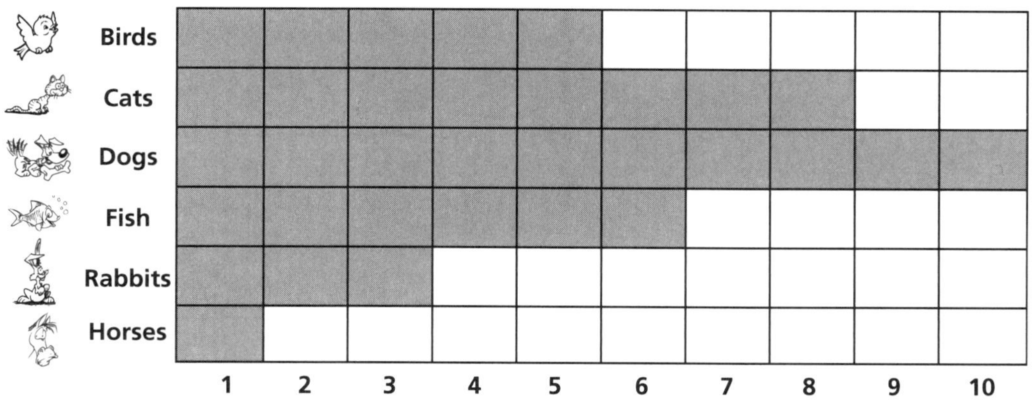

a How many birds? ______

b How many cats? ______

c How many dogs? ______

d How many fish? ______

e How many rabbits? ______

f How many horses? ______

g Which group has the most? ______

h Which group has the least? ______

23:3

0, 2, 4, 6, 8, 10, 12, 14, 16, 18, 20, 22

❶ Join the dots, counting by 2s.

1. The pencil is ____ paperclips long.

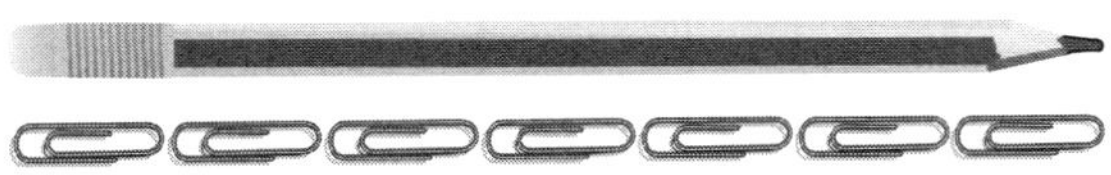

2. 

____

3. The number one more than:

20 ____ 33 ____

4. The month **after** February is

____________.

5. Put a cross on the longer line.

6. Name the shapes used here.

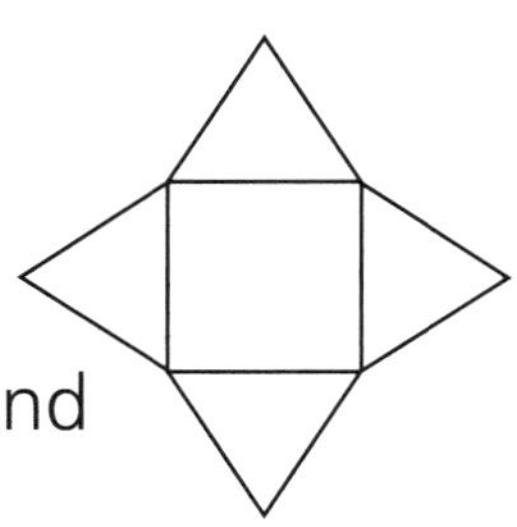

____________ and

____

7. 5 + 6 = ____ 6 + 5 = ____

8. Draw dots, then complete each number sentence.

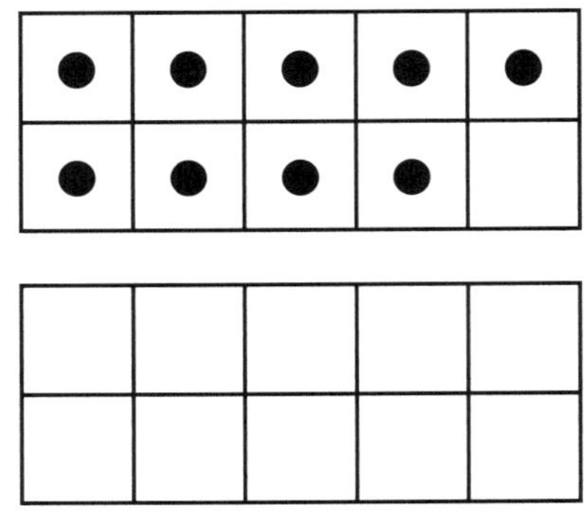

9 + 7 = 9 + ____ + ____

= ____ + ____

= ____

9. Circle the smaller number.

89 or 98

10. Draw a rhombus.

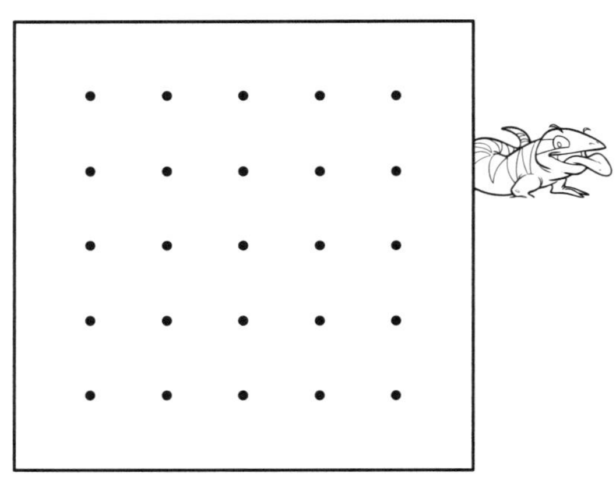

11. Write the number **before** and **after** 39.

	39	

 • *AUSTRALIAN SIGNPOST MATHS 1 MENTALS* • ISBN 978 1 4886 2177 2

24:2

 $\square + \square = \square$

❶ Complete each number sentence.

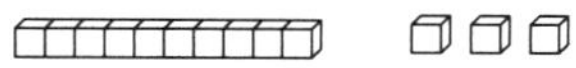 1 ten and 3 ones 10 and 3 = 13	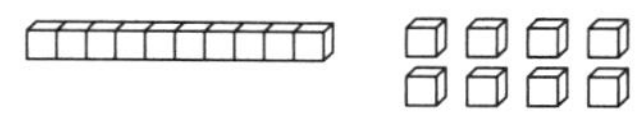 ___ and ___ = ___
 ___ and ___ = ___	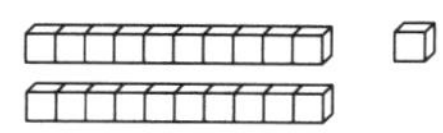 ___ and ___ = ___
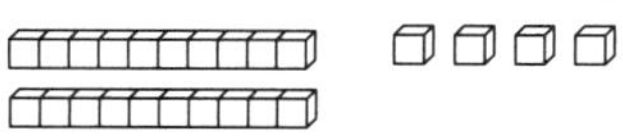 ___ and ___ = ___	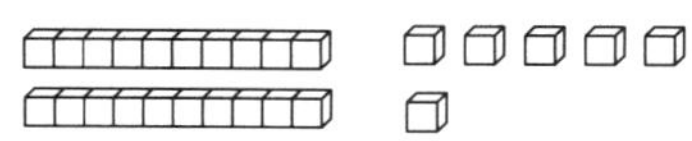 ___ and ___ = ___
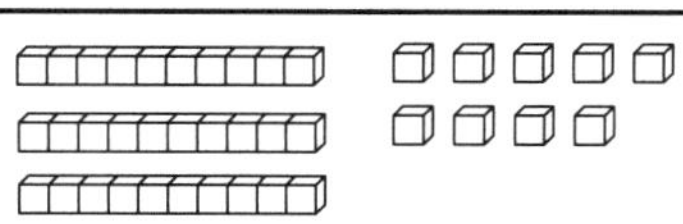 ___ and ___ = ___	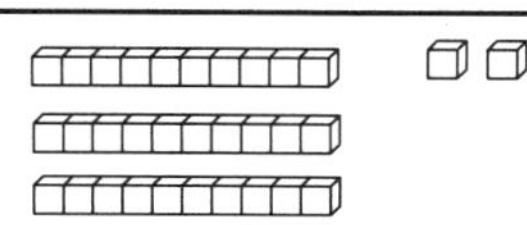 ___ and ___ = ___

❷ Write these numbers in order, starting with the smallest.

82 20 63 31 44

20, ___, ___, ___, ___

24:3

1 3 5 7 9 11 13 15 17 19 21 23

❶ Finish each number pattern.

a 2, 4, ___, 8, ___

b 1, 3, ___, ___, 9

c 10, 8, ___, ___, 2

d 5, 7, ___, ___, 13

e 6, 8, ___, ___, 14

f 9, 7, ___, ___, 1

1 How many blocks would be the same length as the pencil? ______

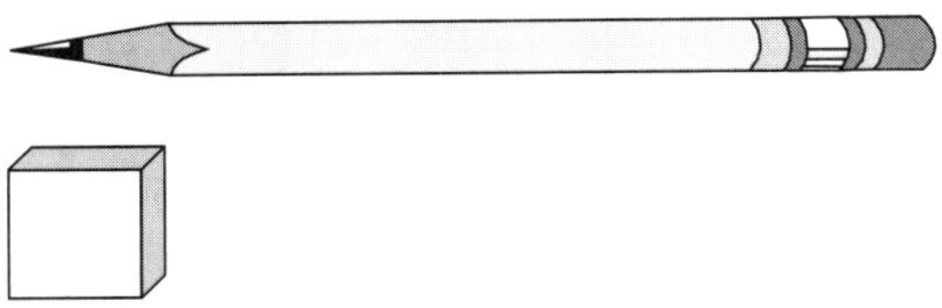

2 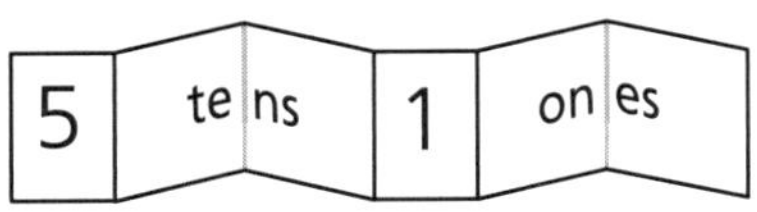

______

3 Finish each number pattern.

a 12, 14, 16, ______, ______

b 5, 10, 15, ______, ______

4 Tick the silver coins.

5 The month **after** April is ______.

6 What number is shown? ______

What number comes next? ______

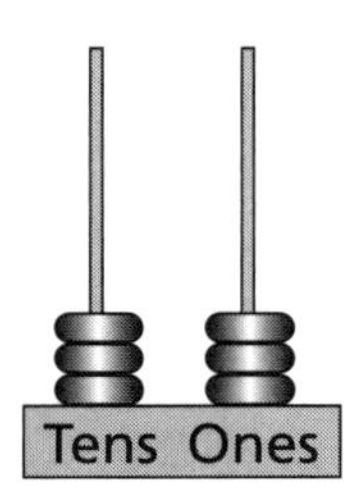

7 Circle the smaller number.

59 or 72

8 63 = ____ tens ____ ones

9 Draw a rectangle.

How many sides? ______

How many corners? ______

10 Write the numeral for:

a seventy-nine ______

b forty ______

c eighty-three ______

11 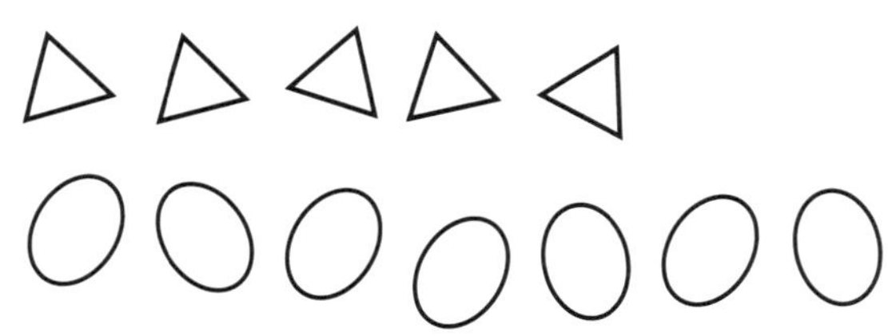

There are ____ more ovals than triangles.

12 Write a number bigger than 90. ______

25:2

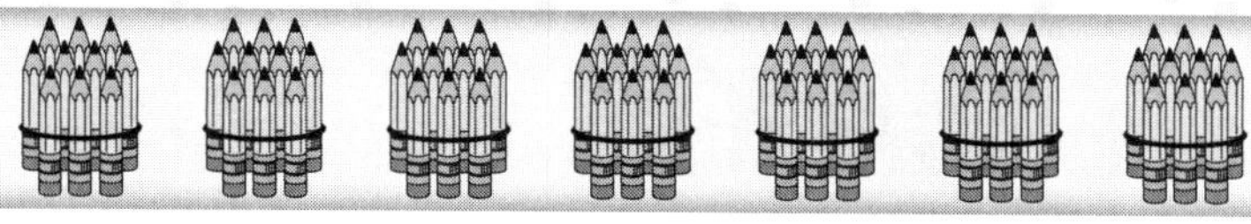

☐ tens = ☐

❶ Complete the numeral expander and then write the number.

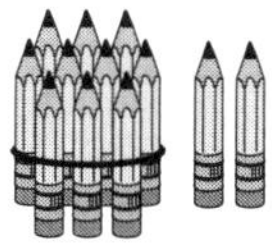

☐ te|ns ☐ on|es

____

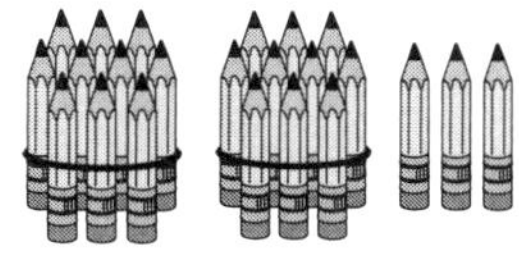

☐ te|ns ☐ on|es

____

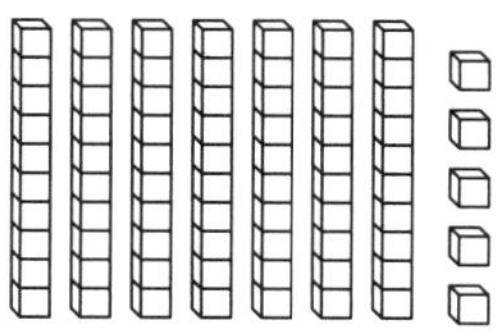

☐ te|ns ☐ on|es

____

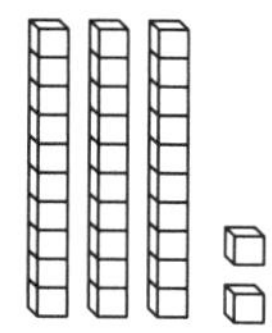

☐ te|ns ☐ on|es

____

❷ Write the months in the correct order.

May *August* *January* *March* *July* *October*
September *June* *November* *February* *April* *December*

1 ________ 2 ________ 3 ________

4 ________ 5 ________ 6 ________

7 ________ 8 ________ 9 ________

10 ________ 11 ________ 12 ________

25:3

30, 40, 50, ______, ______, ______, ______, ______

☐

❸ Complete these number cards.

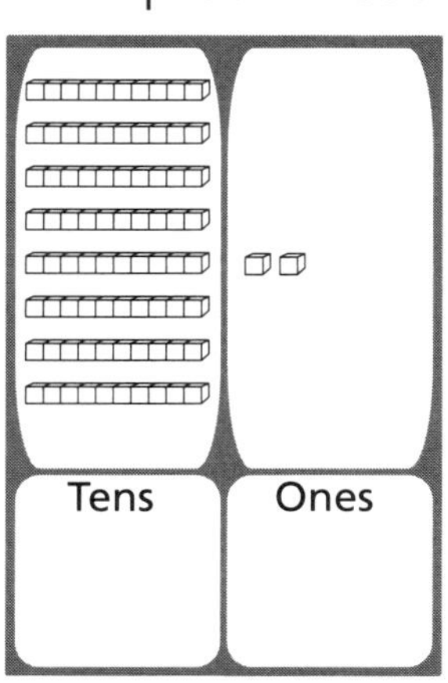

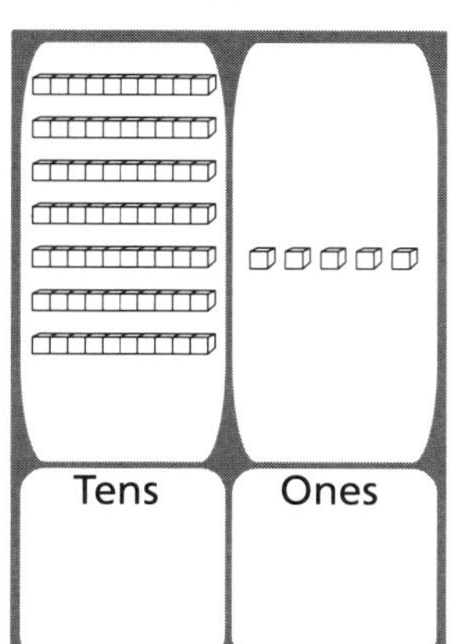

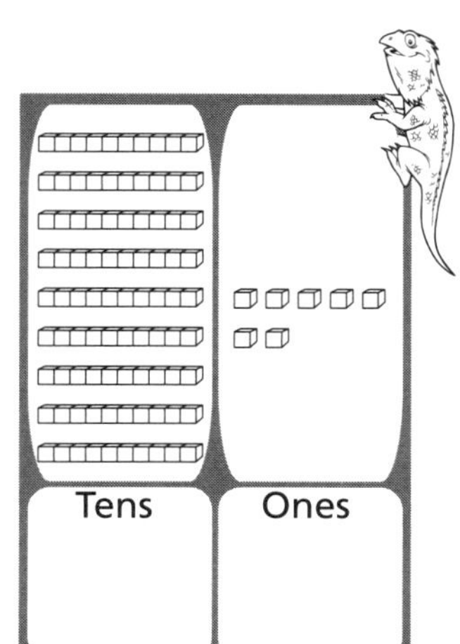

☐

☐

1. 4 tens 7 ones ______

2. Write the number on each abacus.

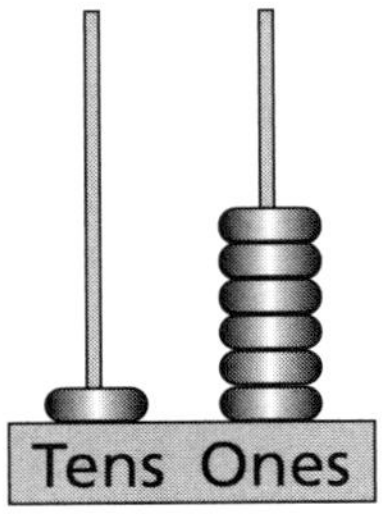

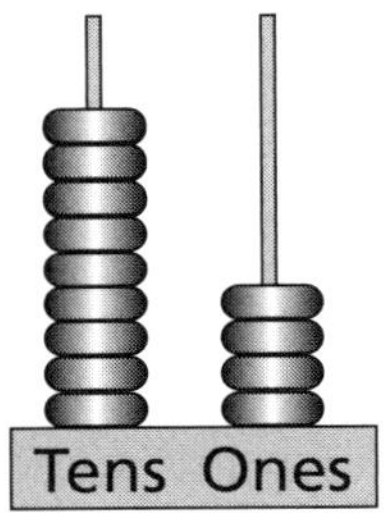

______ ______

3. Which number in Question 2 is larger? ______

4. Finish each number pattern.

a 5, 7, 9, ______, ______, ______

b 0, 3, 6, ______, ______, ______

c 63, 62, 61, ______, ______

5. Fill in the numbers on this clock face.

Show half past 7.

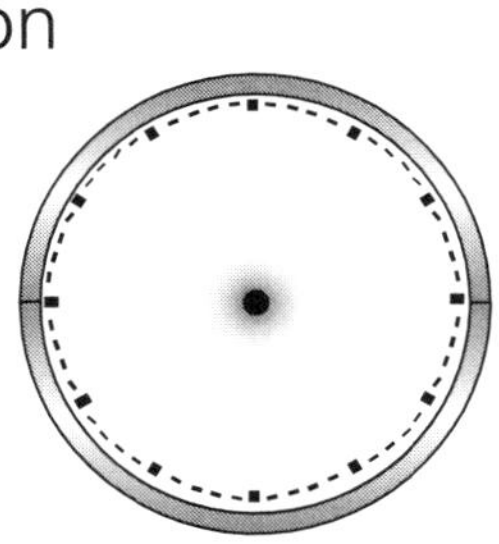

6. 15 take away 5. ______

7. Write the numeral for:

a sixty ______

b twenty-one ______

c one hundred ______

8. 

a How many altogether? ______

Which has:

b the least? ______

c the most? ______

9. 50 = ______ tens ______ ones

10. Count on to add 3.

a 14, ______, ______, ______

so 14 + 3 = ______

b 17, ______, ______, ______

so 17 + 3 = ______

11. Show the digital time.

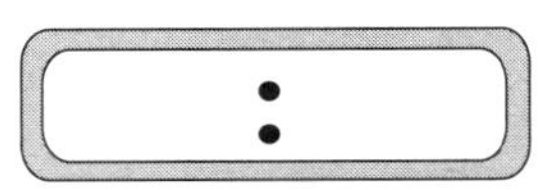

half past 4

12. Fill in the grid.

41		43		
	47		49	

13. The number before 40. ______

 • *AUSTRALIAN SIGNPOST MATHS 1 MENTALS* • ISBN 978 1 4886 2177 2

26:2

January, February, March, April, May, June, July, August, September, October, November, December

❶ In which months do these events happen?

Australia Day  ______

Anzac Day  ______

Christmas  ______

❷ The day **after** Saturday is ______.

1 week = ___ days

❸ The month **after** August is ______.

1 year = ___ months

❹ Circle the pencils that have the same length as the one on the left.

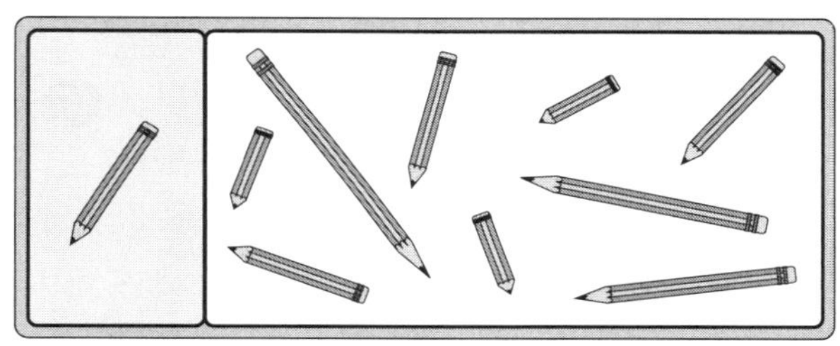

26:3

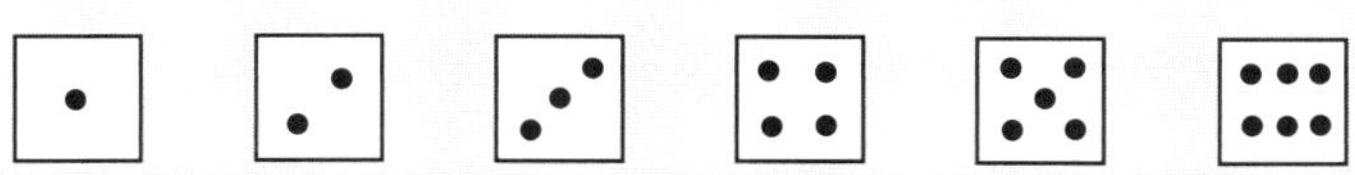

Counting On

❶ How many more are needed to make 5?

4 5

3 + 2 = 5

a 0 + ___ = 5

b 1 + ___ = 5

c 4 + ___ = 5

d 2 + ___ = 5

e 5 + ___ = 5

 • *AUSTRALIAN SIGNPOST MATHS 1 MENTALS* • ISBN 978 1 4886 2177 2

27:1

 +  = ______

❶ What number is shown? ______

Which number is next? ______

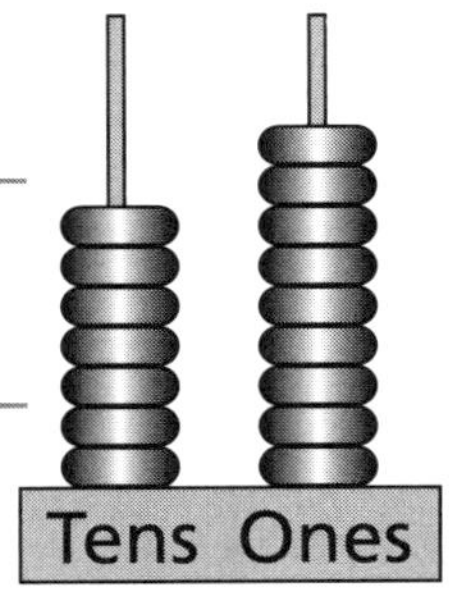

❷ 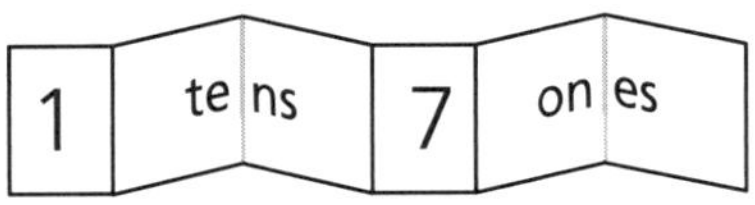

______

❸ Count on to add 2.

a 12, ______, ______

so 12 + 2 = ______

b 15, ______, ______

so 15 + 2 = ______

❹ Write the digital time.

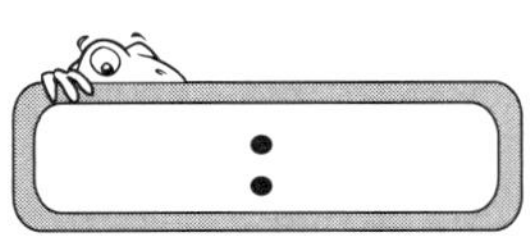

❺ How many more boys than lollies?

______

❻ Finish each number pattern.

a 12 10, 8, ______, ______

b 20, 30, 40, ______, ______

c 5, 7, 9, ______, ______, ______

❼ 44 = ____ tens ____ ones

❽ Show half past 9 on this analogue clock.

❾ Count back to subtract 3.

a 16, ______, ______, ______

so 16 − 3 = ______

b 12, ______, ______, ______

so 12 − 3 = ______

❿ A triangle has ____ sides.

An octagon has ____ sides.

⓫ Circle the model that has the least number of cubes.

⓬ Will a ball:

slide? ______

roll? ______

stack? ______

27:2

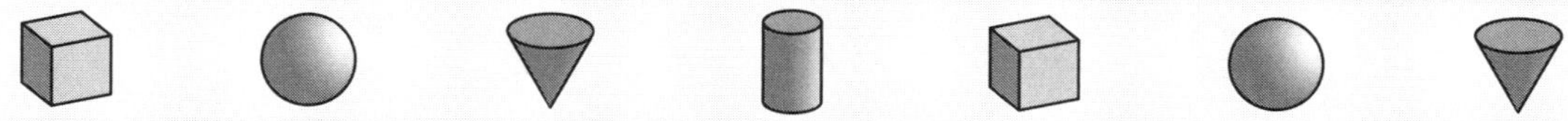

❶

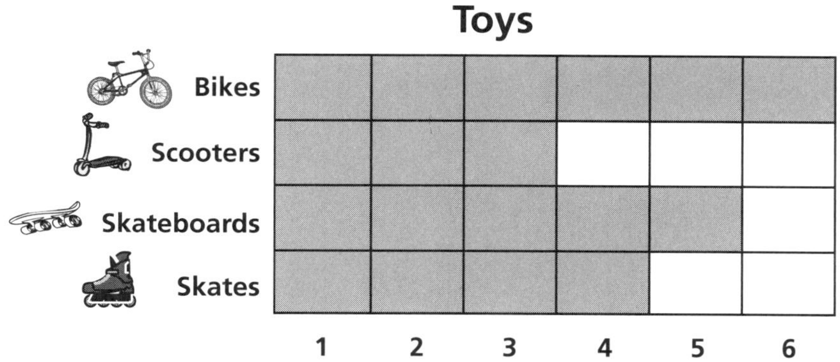

a How many skateboards? ______ 

b How many scooters? ______ 

c How many bikes? ______ 

d How many skates? ______ 

e How many more bikes than scooters? ______

f How many more skateboards than skates? ______

27:3

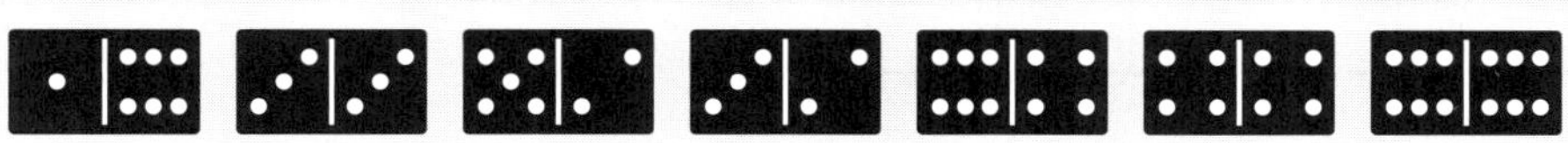

❶ a 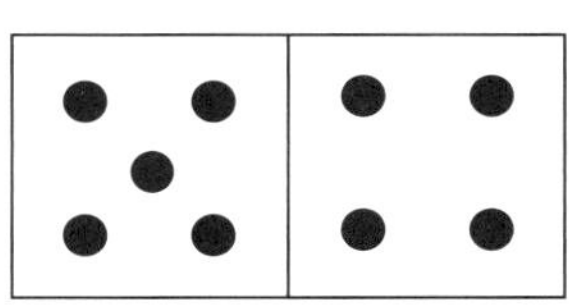 

______ + ______ = ______

b 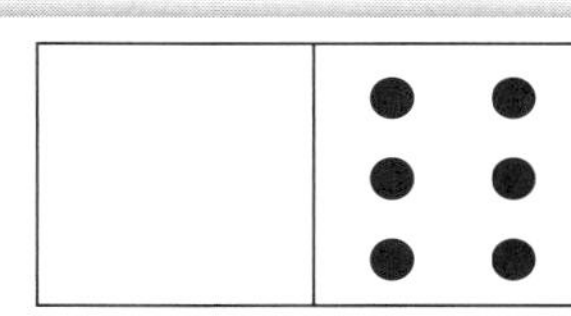

______ + ______ = ______

❷ Say the bigger number first and count on using the dots.

a 5 + 2 = ______

b 4 + 5 = ______

c 6 + 3 = ______

d 1 + 9 = ______

❶ 9 tens 7 ones ______

❷ Write the numeral for:

seventy-three ______

ninety-one ______

❸ On this clock show half past 10.

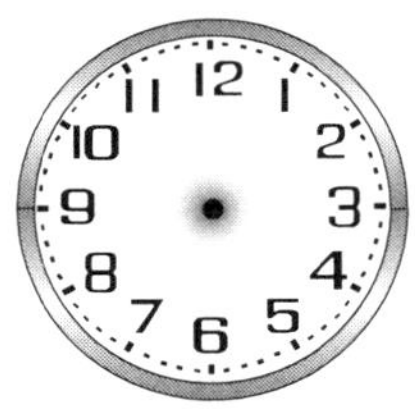

❹ Circle the objects that can stack.

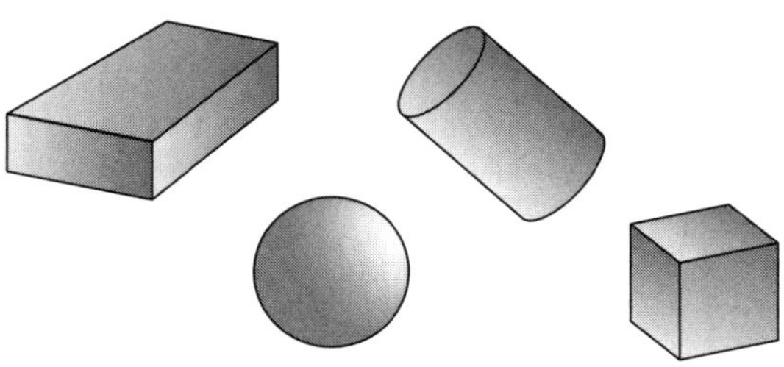

❺

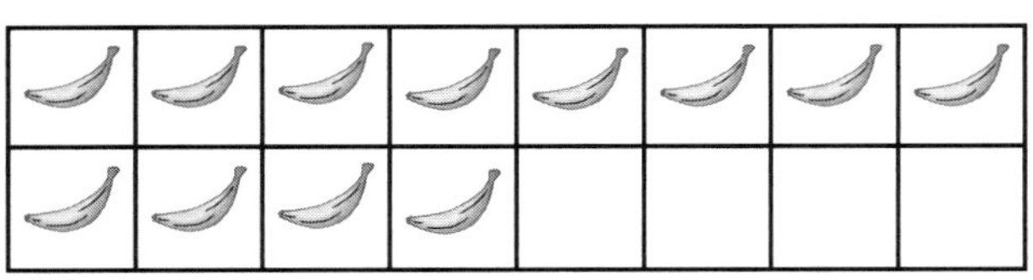

12 + ____ = 16   16 − ____ = 12

❻ Colour one half.

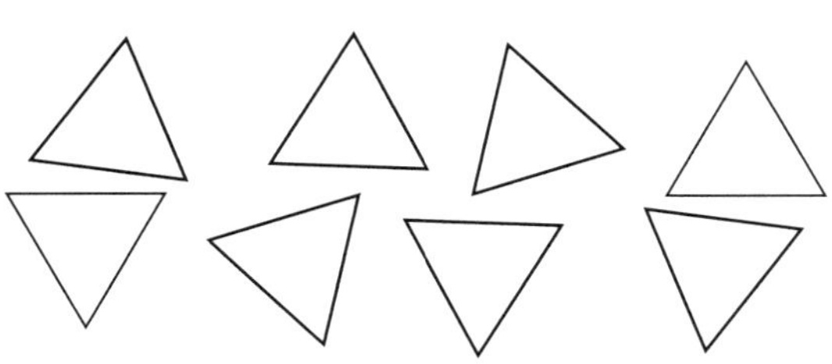

❼ Name something wider than your desk.

______

❽ Count back to subtract 2.

a 15, ______, ______

so 15 − 2 = ______

b 19, ______, ______

so 19 − 2 = ______

❾ This is a h______.

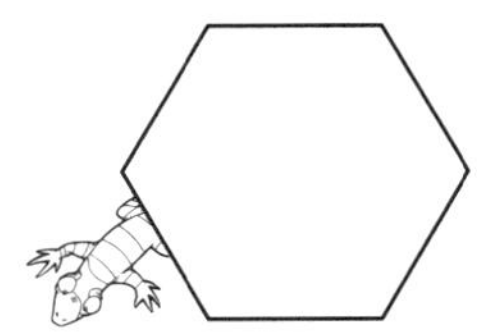

It has ____ sides.

It has ____ corners.

❿ Circle the model with the most cubes.

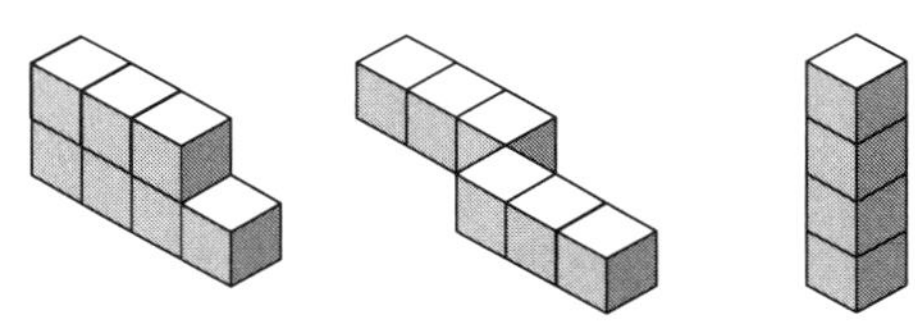

⓫ Scott had 3 balls.
He was given 2 more.

Now, he has ______.

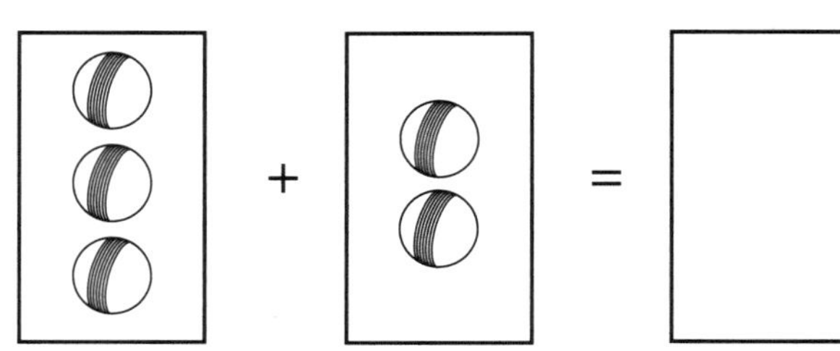

⓬ Write these ordinal numbers.

first ______   third ______

 • *AUSTRALIAN SIGNPOST MATHS 1 MENTALS* • ISBN 978 1 4886 2177 2

28:2

9 – 4 = ☐

❶ Write the missing months.

January, February, ____________, April, ____________, June,
____________, August, September, October, November, ____________

❷ Today is ____________________. Tomorrow is ____________________.

❸ What shapes are on the **left**? ______________________________

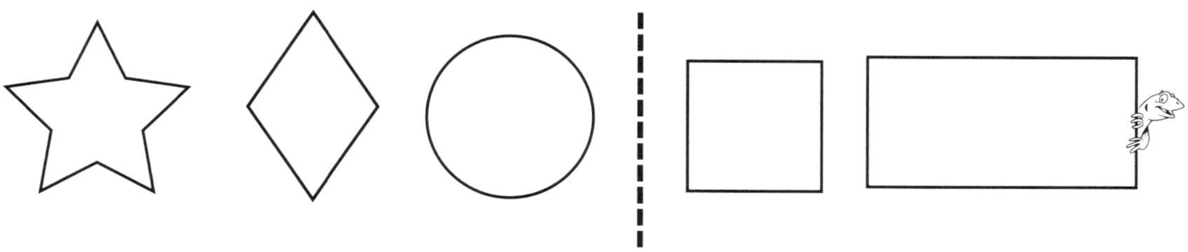

❹ Count on to find the answers.

3 + 2 = ___ 13 + 2 = ___ 8 + 1 = ___ 18 + 1 = ___

5 + 4 = ___ 15 + 4 = ___ 6 + 3 = ___ 16 + 3 = ___

28:3

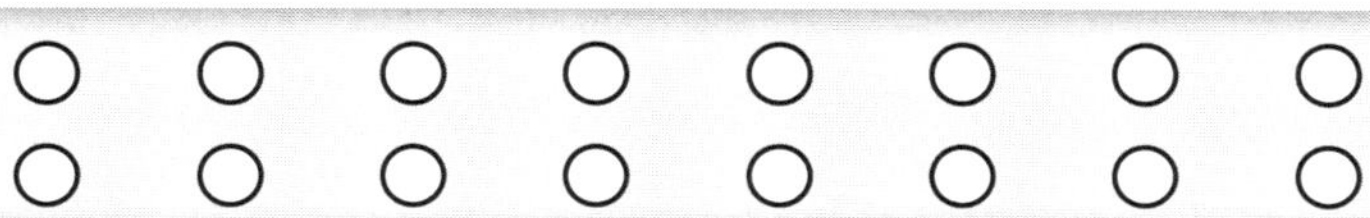

☐

❶ Where do you finish?

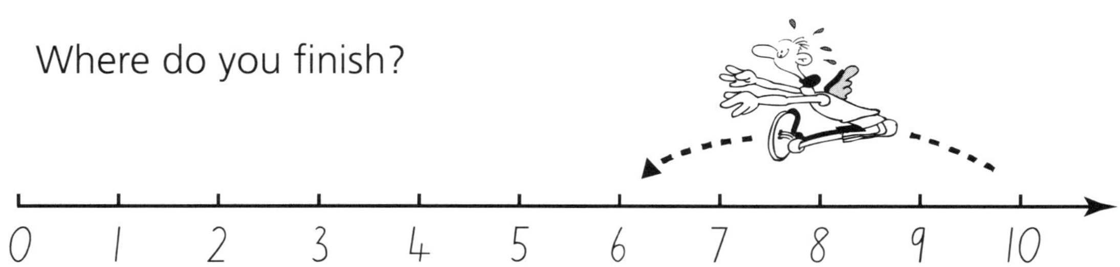

a Start at 10, jump back 4 = 6 **b** Start at 10, jump back 1 = ___

c Start at 10, jump back 6 = ___ **d** Start at 10, jump back 3 = ___

e Start at 10, jump back 9 = ___ **f** Start at 10, jump back 5 = ___

Colour half of each group.

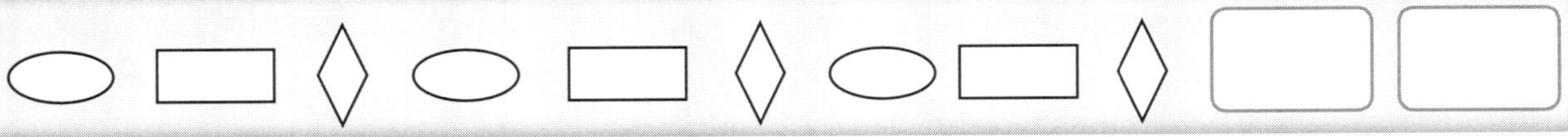

1 Write the digital time for half past 7.

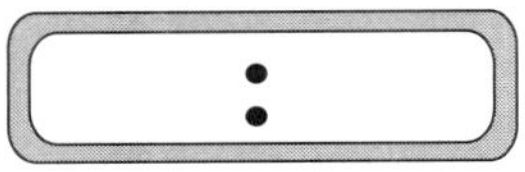

2 How many cubes? ______

3 Lawson had 5 fish.
He was given 2 more.

Now, he has ______.

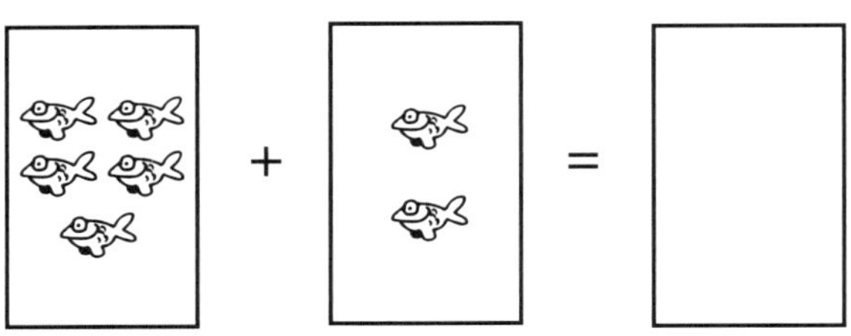

4 Colour one half.

5

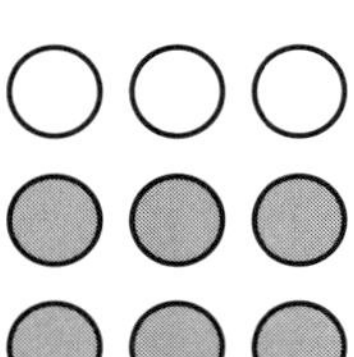

3 + 6 = ______

9 – 3 = ______

9 – 6 = ______

6 22 = ______ tens ______ ones

7 Circle the two shapes that fit together to make a pentagon.

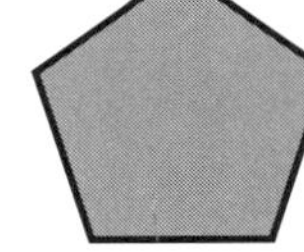

Pentagon

8

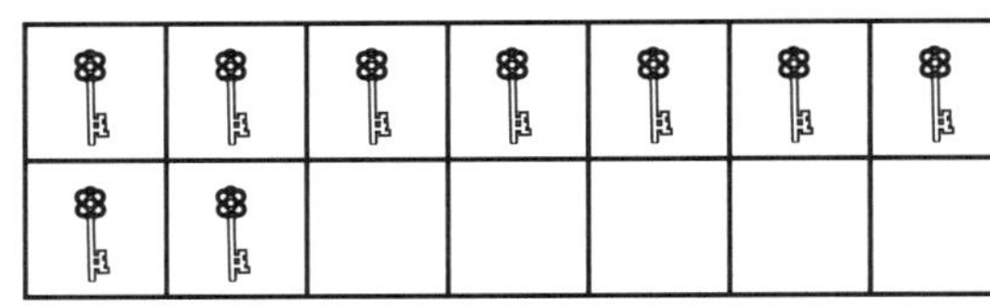

9 + ______ = 14 14 – ______ = 9

9

10 take away 6 equals ______.

10 take away 3 equals ______.

10 take away 8 equals ______.

10 take away 5 equals ______.

10 Circle the larger number.

a 36 or 63

b 90 or 87

11 A bucket holds more than

a ______________________.

 ISBN 978 1 4886 2177 2

29:2

January, February, March, April, May, June, July, August, September, October, November, December

❶ a How many months in one year? ________

b What is the fifth month? ________________

c March is the ________ month.

d What is the last month of the year? ________________________

e What month comes after February? Circle. **June / March**

❷ Circle the stacked objects and write how many in each group.

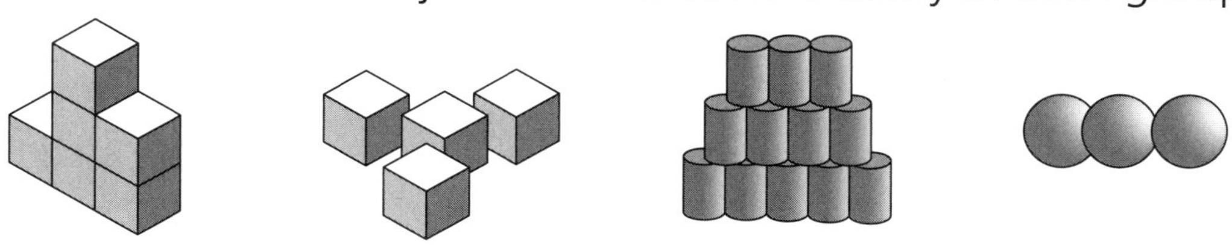

________ ________ ________ ________

❸ Colour the group of 3D objects on the left in Question 2 red.

29:3

☐ – ☐ = ☐

❶ Where do you finish?

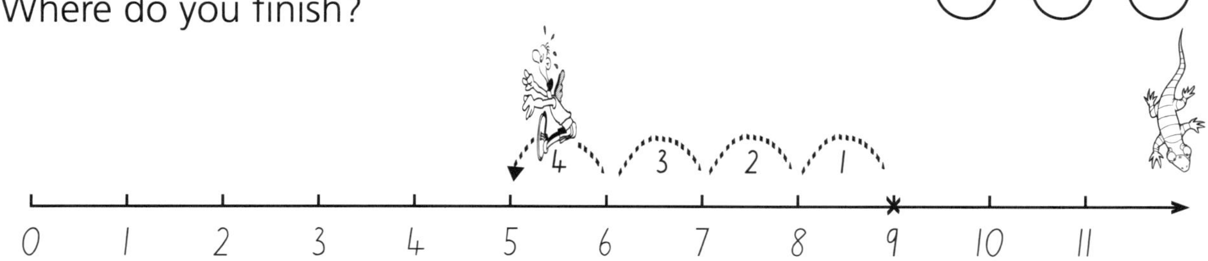

a Start at 9, count backwards 4 = ____

b Start at 9, count backwards 6 = ____

c 9 – 3 = ____ d 7 – 3 = ____ e 8 – 4 = ____ f 11 – 9 = ____

❷ Make a pattern by colouring these circles.

 • • ISBN 978 1 4886 2177 2

☐ - ☐ = ☐

1 

6 + ____ = 10 10 – ____ = 6

2 Circle. It is **likely** / **unlikely** that I will see a crocodile today.

3 Name this shape. 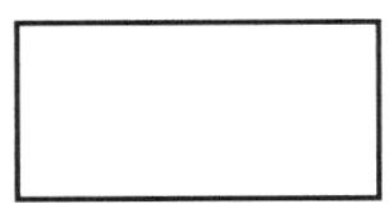

____

4 Write a number smaller than 50. ________

5 Is this balanced, yes or no? ________

6 What number is shown? ________

What number comes next? ______

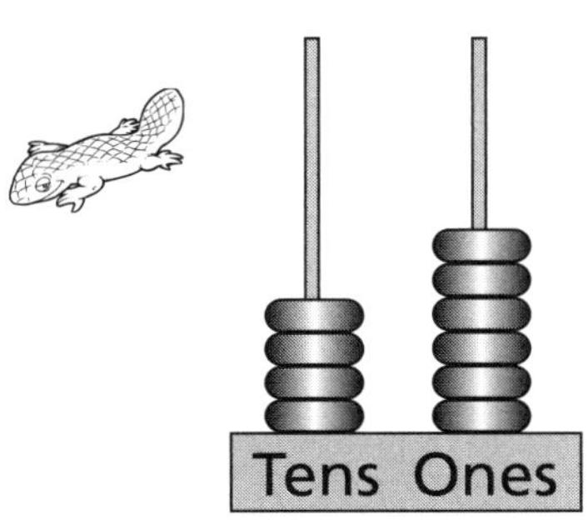

7 | 9 | tens | 0 | ones | = ________

8 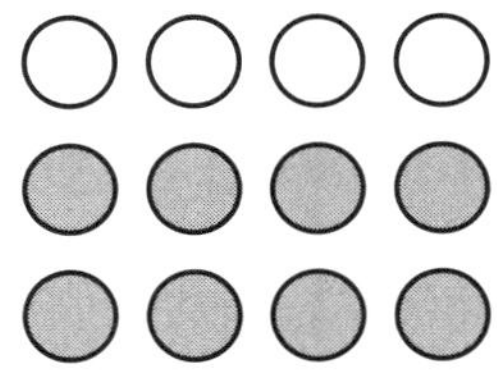

4 + 8 = ________

12 – 4 = ________

12 – 8 = ________

9 Circle the smaller number.

39 or 61

10 Colour the container that holds the most.

Circle the container that holds the least.

11 Put a cross on the container on the left in Question 10.

12 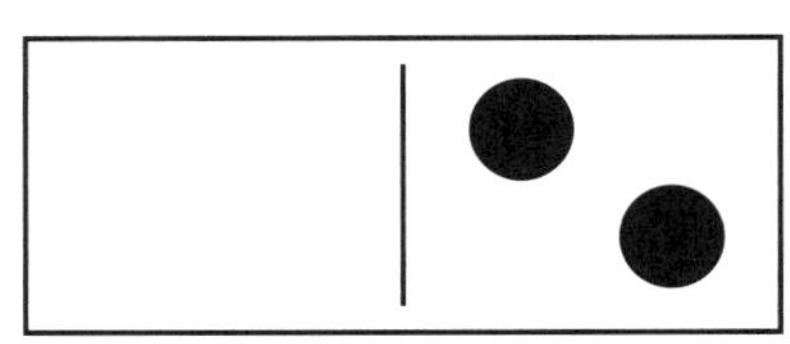 = 6

_____ + _____ = 6

13 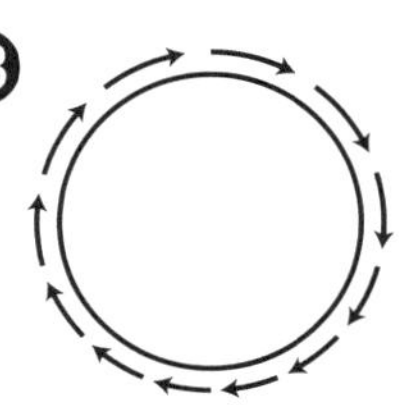 Do these arrows show clockwise or anticlockwise?

____

 ISBN 978 1 4886 2177 2

30:2

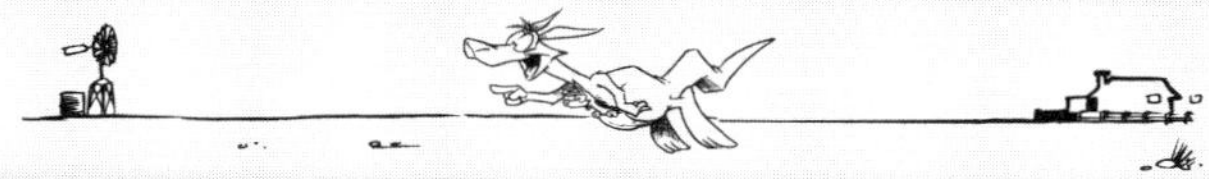

❶ Colour the glass so that it is:

full

half full

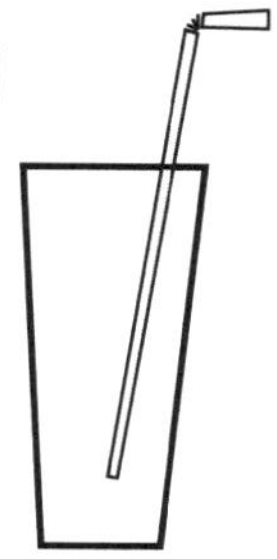

nearly full

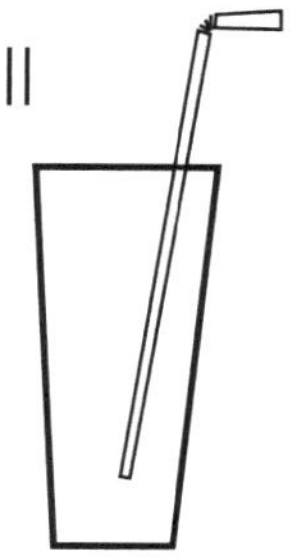

❷ Match each coin to its name.

one dollar   fifty cents   twenty cents   two dollars

❸ Match each note with its name.

$5.00 $10.00 $20.00 $50.00 $100.00

30:3

_____, 24, 25, _____ // 57, 58, _____, _____

❶ Complete these patterns.

a 28, 30, 32, ____, ____

b 63, 61, ____, 57, ____

c 37, 35, ____, 31, ____

d 75, 77, 79, ____, ____

e 44, ____, 48, ____, 52

f 81, 79, 77, ____, ____

❶ 

10 + _____ = 16   16 – _____ = 10

❷ Circle: It is **likely** / **unlikely** that I will see a plane tomorrow.

❸ How many legs altogether? ____

❹ Write the ordinal numbers.

first ______   second ______

third ______   fourth ______

❺ Circle the shape on the left.

❻ Which holds the least? Circle.

❼ | 9 | tens | 3 | ones | = ________

❽ Circle the biggest number.

33   24   61

❾ 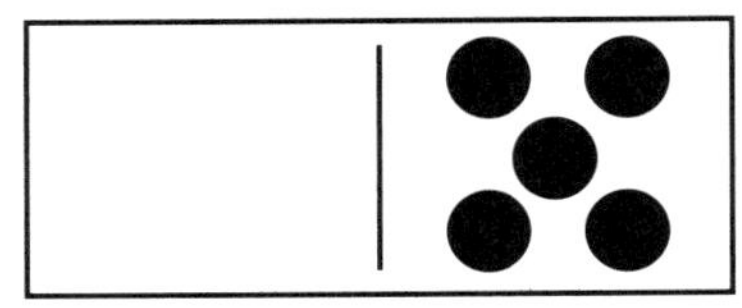 = 9

_____ + _____ = 9

❿ 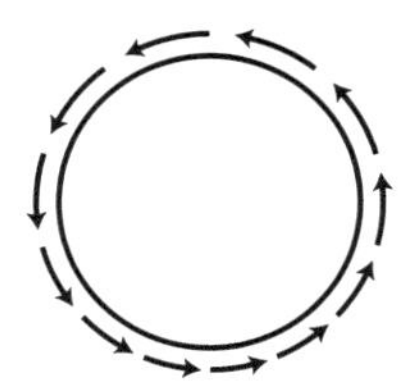

Do these arrows show clockwise or anticlockwise?

____

⓫ **a** 15 – 4 + 4 = ____

b 18 + 5 – 5 = ____

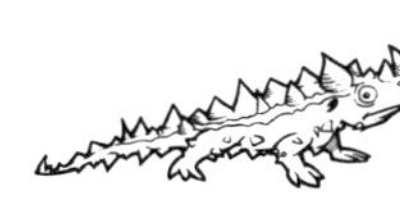

⓬ Circle the 6th hamburger.

Tick the 1st hamburger.

⓭ This month is ________________.

Today is ________________.

 ISBN 978 1 4886 2177 2

31:2

January, February, March, April, May, June, July, August, September, October, November, December

1 **Jo's Timetable**

1 o'clock	pool
2 o'clock	shops
3 o'clock	park
4 o'clock	home
5 o'clock	beach

Where was Jo:

a at 3 o'clock? ______

b at 5 o'clock? ______

c 2 hours after she was at the shops? ______

d 3 hours before she was at home? ______

e 4 hours after she was at the pool? ______

2 Start at the larger number. Count on to add.

3 + 2 = ______ 6 + 3 = ______ 4 + 6 = ______

5 + 4 = ______ 1 + 7 = ______ 1 + 8 = ______

10 + 0 = ______ 2 + 6 = ______ 7 + 3 = ______

3 Write the ordinal numbers.

first ______ second ______ third ______ fourth ______ fifth ______

31:3

 +  ☐ + ☐ = ☐

0 1 2 3 4 5 6 7 8 9 10 11 12 13 14 15 16 17 18 19 20

1 Write the numbers that come 2 before and 2 after:

a ____, 8, ____

b ____, 10, ____

c ____, 3, ____

d ____, 14, ____

e ____, 19, ____

f ____, 12, ____

Total = ☐

❶ Colour the jug that holds the most.

❷ **a** 12 + 7 – 7 = ______

b 16 + 3 – 3 = ______

❸ Circle the lighter side.

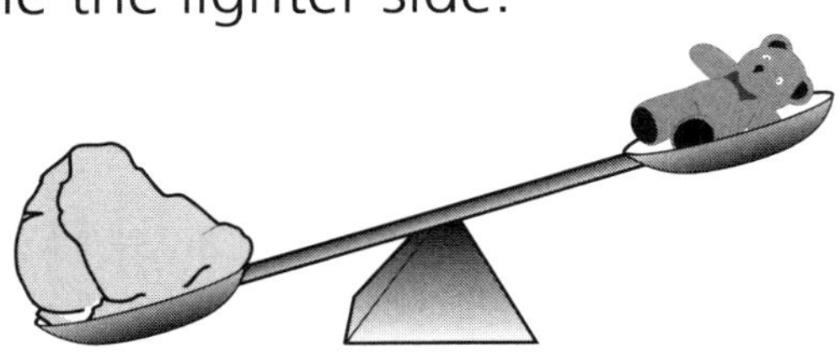

❹ Complete this pattern.

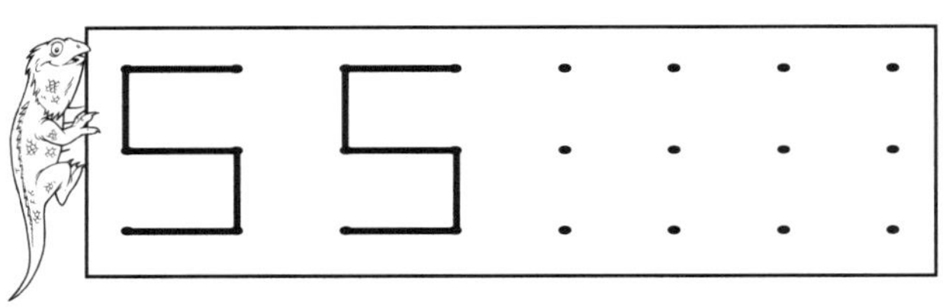

❺ Draw a line to cut each object in half.

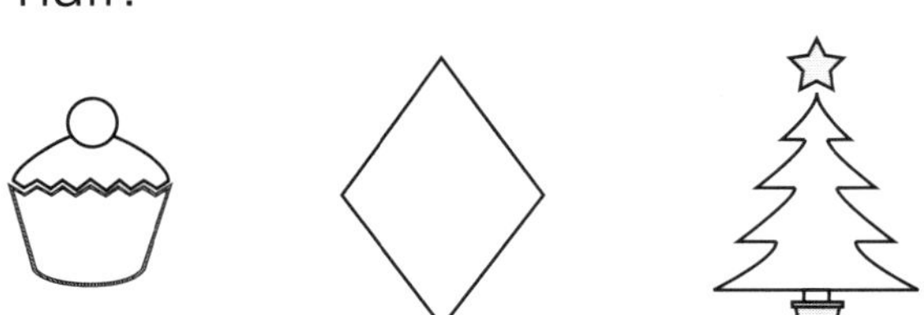

❻ Continue the pattern below.

 ______

❼ | 8 | tens | 8 | ones | = ______

❽ 6 + 4 = ______ 4 + 6 = ______

3 + 7 = ______ 7 + 3 = ______

6 + 1 + 3 = ______

❾ Colour the correct arrow.

❿ 8 + ______ = 15

15 – 8 ______

⓫ Circle the third toy soldier.

⓬ Colour the heavy stones blue.

Tick the light stone.

ISBN 978 1 4886 2177 2

32:2

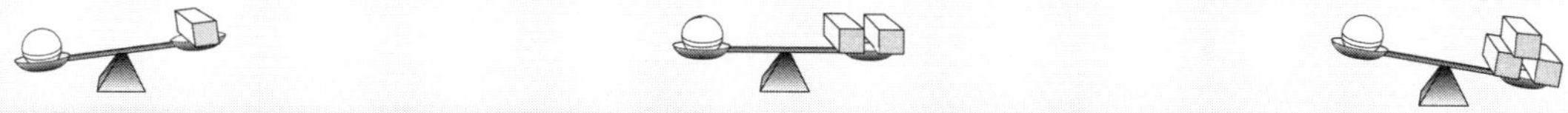

❶ Complete these patterns.

a

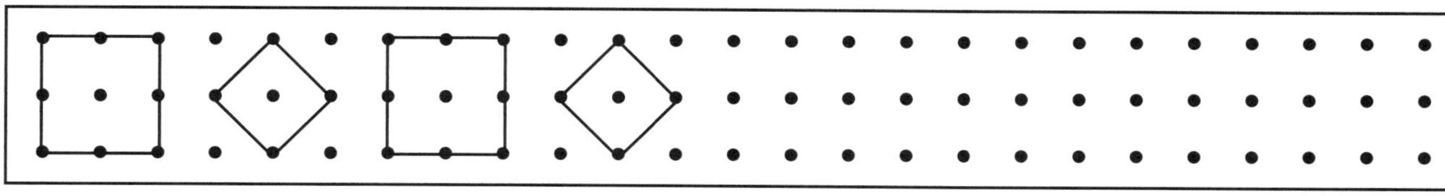

b

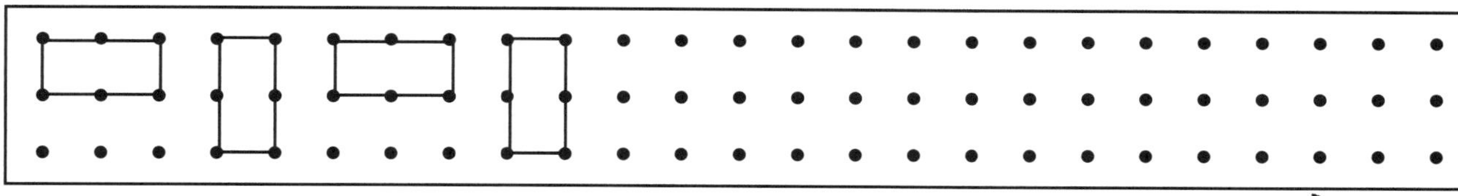

❷

8 – 4 = ____ 9 – 6 = ____ 10 – 5 = ____

3 – 3 = ____ 5 – 0 = ____ 10 – 4 = ____

9 – 2 = ____ 7 – 1 = ____ 10 – 7 = ____

❸ **a** 39 = ____ tens ____ ones **b** 62 = ____ tens ____ ones

32:3

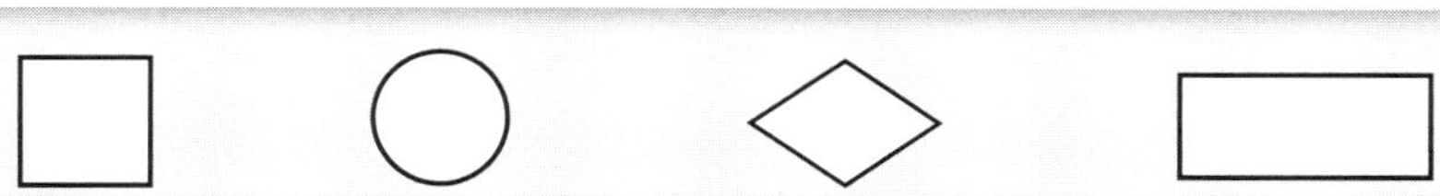

❶ Colour the shapes at the top and copy them at the bottom.

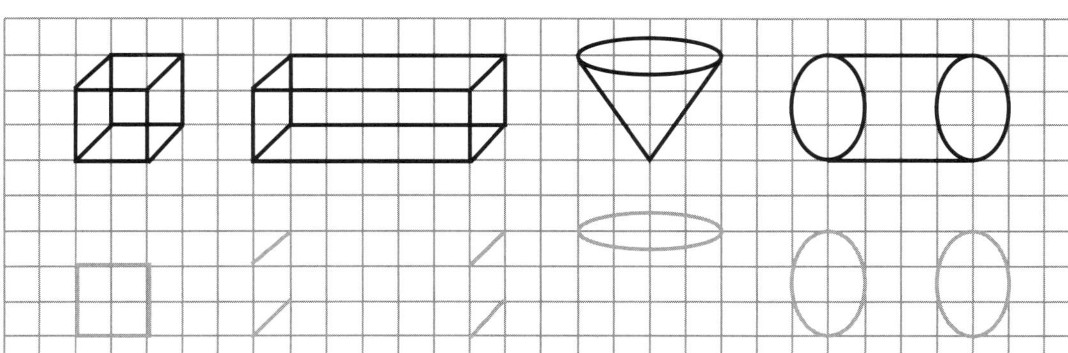

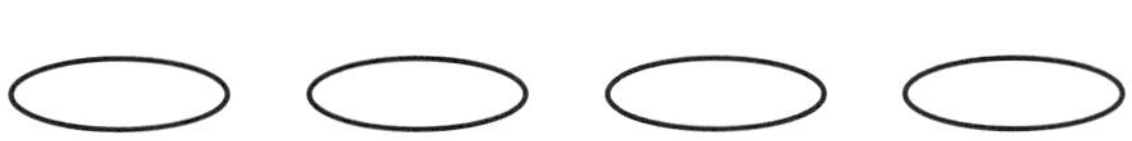

Colour half of each group.

Multiple-choice Questions

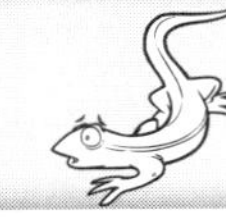

Colour the oval next to the correct answer.

1 This number is:

27

- twenty-two
- twenty-seven
- seventy-two
- thirty-six

2 What number is shown?

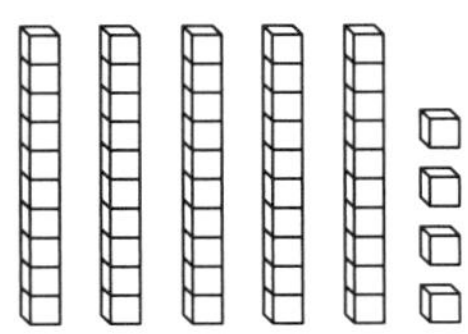

- 46
- 55
- 54
- 24

3 The number before 40 is:

- 29
- 39
- 41
- 40

4 The number 3 more than 5 is:

- 7
- 2
- 8
- 6

5 12 + 2

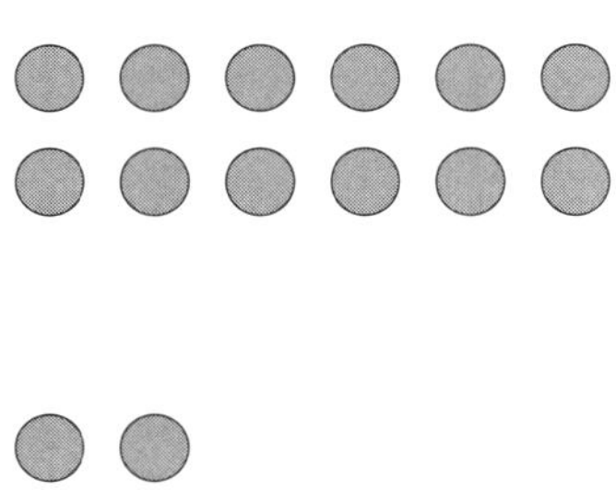

- 14
- 12
- 2
- 10

6 Which square has half shaded?

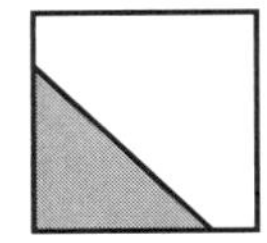
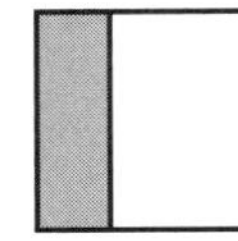
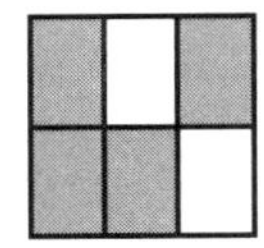
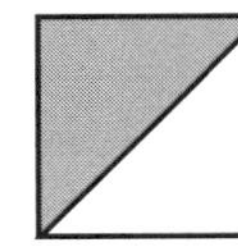

7

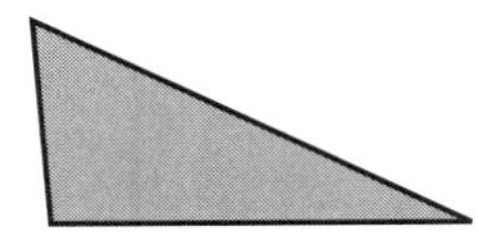

This shape is a:

- square
- circle
- hexagon
- triangle

8

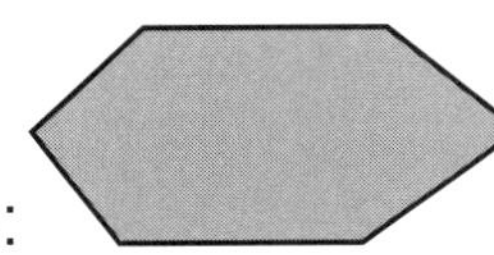

This shape is a:

- square
- circle
- hexagon
- triangle

9

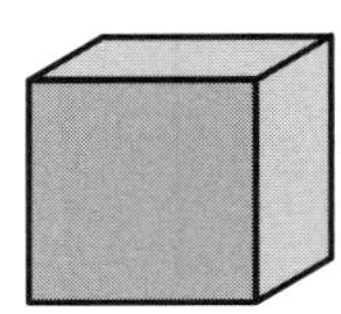

This 3D object is a:

- sphere
- cone
- cube
- cylinder

10 A cat is heavier than a:

- house
- car
- drink bottle
- man

 ISBN 978 1 4886 2177 2

Naming Numbers 0–14

Trace, then write each name and its numeral.

zero		0	
one		1	
two		2	
three		3	
four		4	
five		5	
six		6	
seven		7	
eight		8	
nine		9	
ten		10	
eleven		11	
twelve		12	
thirteen		13	
fourteen		14	

Naming Numbers 15–29

Trace, then write each name and its numeral.

fifteen		15	
sixteen		16	
seventeen		17	
eighteen		18	
nineteen		19	
twenty		20	
twenty-one		21	
twenty-two		22	
twenty-three		23	
twenty-four		24	
twenty-five		25	
twenty-six		26	
twenty-seven		27	
twenty-eight		28	
twenty-nine		29	

Naming Numbers 30–44

Trace, then write each name and its numeral.

thirty		30	
thirty-one		31	
thirty-two		32	
thirty-three		33	
thirty-four		34	
thirty-five		35	
thirty-six		36	
thirty-seven		37	
thirty-eight		38	
thirty-nine		39	
forty		40	
forty-one		41	
forty-two		42	
forty-three		43	
forty-four		44	

 • *AUSTRALIAN SIGNPOST MATHS 1 MENTALS* • ISBN 978 1 4886 2177 2

Naming Numbers 45–59

Trace, then write each name and its numeral.

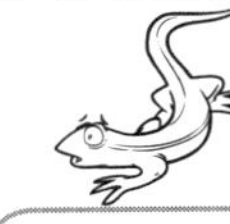

forty-five		45	
forty-six		46	
forty-seven		47	
forty-eight		48	
forty-nine		49	
fifty		50	
fifty-one		51	
fifty-two		52	
fifty-three		53	
fifty-four		54	
fifty-five		55	
fifty-six		56	
fifty-seven		57	
fifty-eight		58	
fifty-nine		59	

Naming Numbers 60–74

Trace, then write each name and its numeral.

sixty		60	
sixty-one		61	
sixty-two		62	
sixty-three		63	
sixty-four		64	
sixty-five		65	
sixty-six		66	
sixty-seven		67	
sixty-eight		68	
sixty-nine		69	
seventy		70	
seventy-one		71	
seventy-two		72	
seventy-three		73	
seventy-four		74	

How Would You Name the Lizards?

1

2

3

4

5

6

7

8

9

10

11

12

13

14

Real names:

1 Horned lizard **2–3** Bearded dragon **4** Gecko **5** Shingleback lizard
6–11 Common garden lizard **12** Blue-tongue lizard **13** Skink
14 Frilled-neck lizard